FORTRESS • 103

THE FORTIFICATIONS OF VERDUN 1874–1917

CLAYTON DONNELL

ILLUSTRATED BY BRIAN DELF

Series editor Marcus Cowper

First published in 2010 by Osprey Publishing,
Midland House, West Way, Botley, Oxford OX2 0PH, UK
44-02 23rd St, Suite 219, Long Island City, NY 11101, USA

E-mail: info@ospreypublishing.com

© 2011 Osprey Publishing Limited

A CIP catalogue record for this book is available from the British Library.

ISBN: 978 1 84908 412 3
E-book ISBN: 978 1 84908 413 0

Editorial by Ilios Publishing Ltd, Oxford, UK (www.iliospublishing.com)
Cartography: Mapping Specialists Ltd.
Page layout by Ken Vail Graphic Design, Cambridge, UK (kvgd.com)
Typeset in Myriad and Sabon
Index by David Worthington
Originated by PDQ Digital Media Solutions, Suffolk, UK
Printed in China through Bookbuilders

11 12 13 14 15   10 9 8 7 6 5 4 3 2 1

Osprey Publishing are supporting the Woodland Trust, the UK's leading woodland conservation charity, by funding the dedication of trees.

www.ospreypublishing.com

Key to military symbols

Army Group, Army, Corps, Division, Brigade, Regiment, Battalion, Company/Battery, Infantry, Artillery, Cavalry, Unit HQ, Engineer, Medical, Navy, Ordnance

Key to unit identification

Unit identifier, Parent unit, Commander
(+) with added elements
(−) less elements

ACKNOWLEDGEMENTS

I would like to thank those people who supported me in writing this book and who helped to make it better. In no particular order, I'd like to thank my wife Donna for her support and encouragement of my 'strange' hobby over the years and for her writing suggestions; my daughter Erin who made ordinary photos into art; my brother Jim for helping to fill some missing gaps and for improving the manuscript; Marcus Massing for information and graphic support; Jean-Pascal Speck for a place to stay and for contacting some folks at Verdun; Julie and Cedric Vaubourg for the beautiful photos and information provided; Marc Romanych for suggestions regarding the manuscript and for his help at the archives; and finally Britt Taylor Collins for his companionship at Verdun and for his prayers, which helped me to finish this work. I would like to dedicate this book to my friend and fortress partner Dan McKenzie, who left this world too soon. I will always miss you Dan.

ARTIST'S NOTE

Readers may care to note that the original paintings from which the colour plates in this book were prepared are available for private sale. All reproduction copyright whatsoever is retained by the Publishers. All enquiries should be addressed to:

Brian Delf
7 Burcot Park
Burcot
Abingdon
OX14 3DH
UK

The Publishers regret that they can enter into no correspondence upon this matter.

COVER IMAGE

© Photos 12/Alamy

THE FORTRESS STUDY GROUP (FSG)

The object of the FSG is to advance the education of the public in the study of all aspects of fortifications and their armaments, especially works constructed to mount or resist artillery. The FSG holds an annual conference in September over a long weekend with visits and evening lectures, an annual tour abroad lasting about eight days, and an annual Members' Day.

The FSG journal FORT is published annually, and its newsletter Casemate is published three times a year. Membership is international. For further details, please contact:
secretary@fsgfort.com
Website: www.fsgfort.com

THE HISTORY OF FORTIFICATION STUDY CENTRE (HFSC)

The History of Fortification Study Centre (HFSC) is an international scientific research organization that aims to unite specialists in the history of military architecture from antiquity to the 20th century (including historians, art historians, archaeologists, architects and those with a military background). The centre has its own scientific council, which is made up of authoritative experts who have made an important contribution to the study of fortification.

The HFSC's activities involve organizing conferences, launching research expeditions to study monuments of defensive architecture, contributing to the preservation of such monuments, arranging lectures and special courses in the history of fortification and producing published works such as the refereed academic journal Questions of the History of Fortification, monographs and books on the history of fortification. It also holds a competition for the best publication of the year devoted to the history of fortification.

The headquarters of the HFSC is in Moscow, Russia, but the Centre is active in the international arena and both scholars and amateurs from all countries are welcome to join. More detailed information about the HFSC and its activities can be found on the website: www.hfsc.3dn.ru
E-mail: ciif-info@yandex.ru

CONTENTS

THE FORTIFICATIONS OF VERDUN 1874–1917

INTRODUCTION

At 0900hrs on 25 February 1916, a small unit of pioneers from Brandenburgisches Infanterie-Regiment 24 of the German III. Armee Korps approached the slopes of the largest and most powerful fort defending Verdun. Four days before, the Germans had begun what would become one of the most gruesome battles of World War I. Led by Feldwebel Kunze, the small squad cut through a barbed-wire obstacle and inched closer and closer to the rim of a 5m-deep ditch that surrounded the superstructure of the fort. Expecting a vigorous French reaction to their presence, they were surprised when no one in the fort noticed them coming. In better times, prior to August 1915, the fort would have been strongly defended by a company of infantry. The approaching Germans would have been spotted by men in steel observation posts and fired on by machine guns in armoured turrets; but not on this day. Tragically, on 25 February 1916, Fort Douaumont, the largest and most powerful fort at Verdun, was defended by only 56 men and captured by less than half that number.

In 1871 France had lost the Franco-Prussian War. The ensuing treaty awarded a significant portion of the provinces of Alsace and Lorraine to Germany. France's new frontier shifted to the west, and the French needed to fortify it as quickly as possible. The fortress of Verdun was a key component of the new border defences. It was developed by the French Army's

Barracks of Fort Douaumont. The fort changed hands three times during the 10-month-long battle. (Author's collection)

Commission des Fortifications, headed by the master military engineer Général Séré de Rivières. He was the driving force behind what would be known as the *barrière de fer* (the 'line of steel'), also known as the Séré de Rivières system, which protected the border and key coastal installations of France.

Construction of the Verdun fortress got under way in 1874. The first fortified positions were built on the sites of former Prussian siege batteries, and over the next 40 years in two concentric rings around the city. The forts were built originally of masonry, the same material used for centuries to build Europe's fortifications. Technological advances in the power, range, and accuracy of artillery during the latter half of the 19th century, however, forced military engineers to turn to concrete and steel as the material for all future fortifications. Construction and modification of the fortifications of Verdun continued until 1914. A second phase of modifications began in 1916, and continued until the end of the war. When World War I began in August 1914, Verdun was among the strongest fortified areas in France.

The Mougin turret for two 155mm guns. Photograph taken in the Schneider-Creusot factory. (National Archives of the US)

Germany's offensive strategy in the west was to sweep through Belgium and encircle the French Army in a rapid pincer movement. The Germans marched for 30 straight days until, exhausted and overextended, their advance was halted on the river Marne and the strategy failed. However, on the way to four years of stalemate on the western front, the Germans pounded the forts of Liège, Namur, Antwerp, and Maubeuge to rubble with their 'secret weapons'; these were powerful 42cm and 30.5cm siege guns – fortress killers, so to speak. The total destruction of Europe's 'ultra-modern' forts quickly transformed France's defensive philosophy and its emphasis upon fortifications as powerful instruments of national defence. Instead, all future tactics would revolve around a well-equipped, offensively minded field

The two-level barracks at Fort la Chaume, on the left bank. The intricately worked masonry façade was not modified with concrete. (Julie & Cedric Vaubourg, www.fortiffsere.fr)

army. As a result of this new direction, the order was given on 6 August 1915 to dismantle the forts and prepare them for destruction. The Army ordered all of Verdun's fortress artillery pieces, except those permanently mounted in fixed armoured turrets, to be removed and the fortress troops attached to the field army. This decision would have serious consequences in the battle soon to take place at Verdun.

Meanwhile, in late September 1914, the German Army made an unsuccessful attempt to break through the French lines along the river Meuse. However, they did succeed in capturing a small bridgehead at Saint-Mihiel south of Verdun. Verdun was now surrounded on three sides and vulnerable to being completely cut off, but safe for the time being. The year 1915 was relatively quiet for the fortress until August, when the dismantlement of the forts commenced. Thus, it was a very different and weakened fortress the Germans encountered in February 1916.

It is highly probable that this weakness contributed to the German decision to choose Verdun as the place for their 1916 offensive; after all, events taking place there throughout the fall of 1915 must have been observed and reported by German agents. Plus, Verdun's lines of communications had been reduced to a single road leading to the south-west. Strategically, the French Army believed it was doing the right thing, but, as the battle progressed, events proved that the decision to reduce the forts was a bad one. The importance of the forts, not only as patriotic symbols but superb observation posts and strongholds, was recognized once again. Général Pétain, placed in command of the fortress early in the battle, ordered the forts to be returned to fighting strength. This act played a large part in the ultimate French survival and victory at Verdun.

Depending on one's perspective, the French victory resulted either from a brilliant strategy on the part of the French generals, or a series of monumental blunders by the Germans. In reality, the outcome was a combination of both, with the forts playing a major role in both victory and defeat. To the French, the forts were a daily reminder and visible objective to fight for, and they proved to be the final undoing of the German offensive. In the months after its capture in February 1916, Fort Douaumont's distant heights stood as a driving force for the French Army. The fighting that took place in the tunnels of Fort Vaux, a stubborn defence led by Major Raynal that ended only after the drinking water ran out, serves as an example of France's tenacity in holding on to the last square centimetre of lunar landscape that Verdun became, to the last man if necessary. The words of Général Coutanceau, military governor of the fortress from 1912 to 1915, sum up the spirit of the fortress troops: 'Better to be buried under the ruins of a fort than to surrender it.' The battle demonstrates both the extraordinary power of a fort to inflict massive losses on an attacker and the serious consequences that can ensue by allowing the enemy to seize too easily such a powerful weapon.

No history of the battle of Verdun is complete without discussing the primary role the fortifications played in the final outcome of the battle. Because of Verdun, the tide towards the value of fortifications once again turned in their favour, greatly influencing the crucial decisions of the 1920s that would produce the Maginot Line. The subject would be hotly debated after the war, but the generals who observed the battle and lived the slogan 'They shall not pass', especially Général Pétain, would never forget what the battered concrete, twisted steel and dark dust-filled tunnels meant to the soldiers who fought at Verdun, and their critical role in the French endgame.

CHRONOLOGY

13 September 1873
Occupation forces from the new German Empire leave Verdun after victory in the Franco-Prussian War of 1870–71. France loses Alsace and part of Lorraine.

1874
France embarks on an ambitious programme of fortifying its new border with Germany. Building work begins on a major fortress at Verdun.

3 August 1914
Declaration of war – France is officially at war with Germany.

4–24 August 1914
The Belgian fortresses of Liège and Namur fall to the Germans after heavy bombardment that destroys the concrete forts.

August–September 1914
German 42cm siege cannon pound the fortresses of Lille, Longwy and Maubeuge. All three fall to the Germans.

24 September 1914
German forces capture a bridgehead over the river Meuse at Saint-Mihiel. Verdun is isolated on three sides.

5 August 1915
All field guns in the forts and batteries of Verdun are removed. Explosive charges are placed to destroy the forts in case of a German attack.

21 February 1916
The Germans launch a massive assault on the Verdun salient.

25 February 1916
Fort Douaumont, the largest Verdun fort, falls to the Germans without a fight.

7 June 1916
Fort Vaux falls during a major German offensive to capture the right bank of the Meuse above Verdun.

23 June 1916
The German offensive stumbles in front of the Ouvrage de Froideterre.

11 July 1916
A final German offensive is launched. At Fort Souville, German troops reach the ditch and can see the town of Verdun for the first time, but their advance is halted.

24 October 1916
French forces launch a general counter-attack – Fort Douaumont is recaptured.

18 December 1916
The French offensive ends. All land taken by the Germans since February is back under French control.

1917
A massive modernization effort is undertaken to construct secure tunnels and shelters below the existing forts. The work continues throughout the year.

September 1918
The American Expeditionary Force under General Pershing launches the Meuse–Argonne offensive, which pushes the Germans out of the area to the north of Verdun and ends with the Armistice of 11 November.

1930–40
Moderate repairs and modifications are made to the forts of Verdun. Forts Vaux and Douaumont are incorporated into the Maginot Line.

15 June 1940
Verdun surrenders to German forces with hardly a shot fired.

DESIGN AND DEVELOPMENT

Verdun's role as a key defensive position goes back more than 1,500 years. For centuries it has guarded both the passage of the river Meuse and the main road from Paris to Metz. In fact, its name stems from the Latin 'Vir Dunum', or 'fortress on the river'. The city has endured a total of 11 sieges, including Attila the Hun's in AD 450. King Louis XIV's fortress engineer, Vauban, built the bastioned system and citadel that currently surrounds the town. Because of improvements in artillery in the 1860s, central redoubts like the citadel became vulnerable to long-range artillery bombardment, so Europe's military engineers began building systems of detached forts around the perimeter of their most strategic cities. Général Séré de Rivières, France's '19th-century Vauban', began to build detached forts around the city of Metz in 1867, but three years later German forces invaded and defeated France in the Franco-Prussian War. The Germans took possession of the provinces of Alsace and Lorraine, changing France's entire defensive strategy, particularly at Verdun.

On 16 September 1873 the last German occupying troops left Verdun. France was now faced with a new and defenceless border. Meanwhile, on the opposite side of the border, the Germans had a two-year head start on construction of the great fortress at Metz. The French Comité de Défensé (Committee of Defence) was formed in 1872 to study the problem and plan for the defences of the new border. Général de Rivières was named Secretary of the Committee and quickly became the driving force for its direction and the works it produced. He played a major role in developing the technical criteria for the new fortifications. For political reasons Général de Rivières eventually left the Committee, but his name is forever linked to the hundreds of fortifications built throughout France from 1874 to 1914, including the most powerful fortress of all – Verdun.

The new fortifications were developed according to a systematic plan by the French Corps du Génie (Engineer Corps). The initial stage consisted of locating the optimum sites for the main fortifications. Plans were then drawn up to include the objectives of the works, such as the key lines of communication that needed to be defended and dangerous positions where enemy artillery might be sited. The engineers worked closely with the artillerymen to plot the best location for each fort's guns. Once the plan was completed, it was passed to the Brigade Topographique (Topographic Brigade) to perform terrain soundings for site excavation and the construction of access routes. The parcels of land upon which the forts were to be built were then acquired. The final project dossier would include a description of the mission of each particular fortification and a detailed cost estimate. Architectural plans were drawn up, which included the surface and sub-surface elements. Finally, after approval, the scope of work was written up and submitted to private building contractors for bidding.

The contractors hired workers from the local areas. Nearby quarries provided stone to build the forts. Narrow-gauge 60cm railway track was laid to transport materials to the building site. Inclined planes were built to haul materials up the steep slopes, using pulleys or locomotives that pulled small wagons to the construction sites.

In the meantime, the Commission d'Armements (Armaments Commission) studied the attack conditions of each fort and drew up a report detailing the 'state of armament' required for fulfilment of the fire mission. Engineers and artillery specialists who had earlier determined the best positioning of the guns on the ramparts now worked out the quantity of ammunition needed per

The fortifications of Verdun

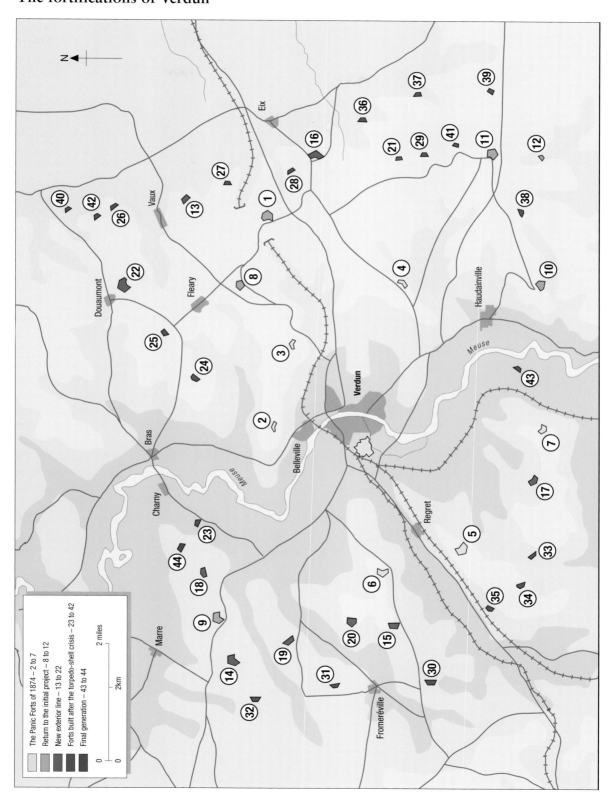

Legend:
The Panic Forts of 1874 – 2 to 7
Return to the initial project – 8 to 12
New exterior line – 13 to 22
Forts built after the torpedo-shell crisis – 23 to 42
Final generation – 43 to 44

At the centre of Verdun is the citadel, built by Vauban in 1670. The barracks are in the centre. (National Archives of the US)

artillery piece, and the armaments were then placed on order with factories or supply depots.

The initial plan for the Verdun project called for two lines of fortifications on the heights of the right and left banks of the Meuse, with smaller gun batteries to guard the passage of the river Meuse through Verdun. In 1874 the groundbreaking act for the fortress of Verdun took place at what would become Fort Tavannes. No sooner had work begun when a diplomatic disagreement between France and Germany arose that threatened to ignite another war. The order was given to begin the emergency construction of six small redoubts on the hills immediately overlooking the city, approximately 2.5–6.5km from the old Vauban fortress. Ironically, the sites chosen were the locations used by the Prussians to set up siege batteries in 1792 and 1870, and eventually become known as the 'Forts de la Panique' ('Panic Forts').

On the right bank, redoubts were built on the heights of Belleville, Saint-Michel and near the quarry of Belrupt. On the left bank Forts Dugny, Regret and La Chaume were built. They were not yet designated 'forts' (that

Initial project and the 'Forts de la Panique', December 1874 to February 1875								
Name	Construction date	Modernization date	Total cost (francs)	Men	Machine-gun turrets	75mm turrets	155mm turrets	Armoured observatories
1 – Tavannes	1874	1889–90	2.5 million	761				
2 – Belleville	1875	n/a	536,000	164				
3 – Saint-Michel	1875	n/a	450,000	160				
4 – Belrupt	1875	n/a	1.6 million	298				
5 – Regret	1875	1906–09	2.6 million	132	2	2		4
6 – La Chaume	1875	n/a	1.3 million	208				
7 – Dugny	1875	1901–02 1902–08	2.2 million	252	2	1		3
The number preceding each fort's name corresponds to the location indicated on the map on p. 9								

would happen later); they were large gun batteries with parapets for infantry defence and ramparts for the guns on top, with protection for the soldiers in masonry shelters below ground. The redoubts were trapezoidal in shape and surrounded by a dry ditch defended by caponiers – casemates of one or two storeys in height for rifles and small cannon that were built across the ditch. The ditch casemates in both the redoubts and the forts were defended by rapid-firing cannon. The Reffye seven-calibre model was originally selected but was later switched to the 12-Culasse Model 1884. The 12-Culasse was a shortened 12-calibre front-loading gun used in the field with a Lahitole-model breech

A flanking casemate with a revolving cannon on the left and a 12-calibre rapid-fire gun (12-Culasse) on the right. (Julie & Cedric Vaubourg, www.fortiffsere.fr)

mechanism affixed to the back end. The shorter barrel fitted inside the casemate and the breech increased the rate of fire. With a range of 3,400m and a high velocity of 288m per second, it fulfilled the dual role of ditch defence and flanking fire. It could fire a standard shell as well as grapeshot containing 192 balls, and was an excellent anti-personnel gun. Later, the defences of the redoubts were upgraded and they were officially designated as 'forts'.

After the threat of war subsided, construction resumed on the original Séré de Rivières project. Forts Souville, Marre, Haudainville, Rozelier and Bois Réunis were completed in 1879 and the last two received their armaments that same year. No additional work was planned.

In 1879 Germany and Austria-Hungary formed a diplomatic and military alliance. Italy joined in 1882 to form the Triple Alliance. This led to a vigorous building programme that started in 1881 to expand the number of fortifications at Verdun. Several new forts were added – Vaux and Bois-Bourrus in 1881, and Moulainville and Landrecourt in 1883. In addition, smaller fortifications called 'posts' were built at Sartelles, Belle-Épine, Chana, Choisel and Croix-Brandier. From 1881 to 1891 a total of 34 interval gun batteries were added to augment and disperse the firepower of the main forts. These were originally constructed as fieldworks, and would later become permanent structures. Most importantly, the construction of Fort Douaumont began in 1885. By 1886 the Verdun fortress consisted of ten forts, six redoubts and five posts along an inner and outer ring 3–9km out from the town centre.

Return to the initial project, July 1875								
Name	Construction date	Modernization date	Total cost (francs)	Men	Machine-gun turrets	75mm turrets	155mm turrets	Armoured observatories
8 – Souville	1875	1888–89 1990–91	2.65 million	314			1	
9 – Marre	1875	1888–89 1905–06	2.5 million	426	1			1
10 – Haudainville	1876	1900–02	2.4 million	243	2			2
11 – Rozelier	1877	1890–01 1902–13	4.5 million	605	3		1	2
12 – Bois-Réunis	1878	n/a						

The ditch of Fort Douaumont. This is the left front lateral looking towards the north-east casemate (right centre) where Feldwebel Kunze's pioneers entered the fort on 24 February 1916. The escarp is to the right and the counterscarp to the left. At the edge of the frame are vestiges of the former counterscarp wall and defensive iron grille. (Author's collection)

In 1887 a series of interval infantry works (*ouvrages*) was built between the forts. The mission was to assure mutual defence between the forts – to complete the link, so to speak. They were smaller in size than the forts, ranging from 105m by 85m (Saint-Symphorien) to 175m by 110m (Déramé). Some were equipped with machine-gun turrets and two had 75mm turrets. Several were modified in the early 1900s. They were surrounded by a shallower ditch with a barbed-wire obstacle and no flanking casemates for protection.

Everything done up to this point would be put to the test when, in 1886, a new type of explosive charge was invented that made all fortifications built to this point obsolete. The *crise de l'obus-torpille*, or 'torpedo-shell crisis', was the result of the invention of a new type of explosive material called picric acid used inside artillery shells to increase their explosive force. To understand the true impact of the new shell on masonry fortifications, it is also important to take a quick look at the development of artillery since the 1850s.

In the mid-1850s, the Krupp armaments firm in Germany designed a new type of gun barrel with a set of parallel grooves etched in a spiral pattern on the inside surface of the barrel. This process was called 'rifling' and the spiral grooves caused the shell, now in the shape of a bullet (or 'torpedo'), to fly a

New exterior line – Threats from the alliance between Germany, Austria-Hungary and Italy								
Name	Construction date	Modernization date	Total cost (francs)	Men	Machine-gun turrets	75mm turrets	155mm turrets	Armoured observatories
13 – Vaux	1881	1888–95 1904–06 1910–12	2.9 million	298		1		3
14 – Bois-Bourrus	1881	1891–94 1904–07 1913–14	2.95 million	290	3			2
15 – Sartelles	1881	1894–97 1904–06	1.1 million	115	2			2
16 – Moulainville	1883	1889–91 1905–09	3.65 million	250	2	1	1	4
17 – Landrecourt	1883	1891 1904–06	2.75 million	300	2	1		3
18 – Belle-Épine	1883	n/a	400,000	88				
19 – Choisel	1883	1894–97 1906–12	1.3 million	290	2	1		3
20 – Chana	1883	1906–11	1.15 million	150		1		1
21 – Croix-Brandier	1883	n/a						
22 – Douaumont	1885	1887–89 1901–03 1907–09 1911–13	6.1 million	890	2	1	1	4

Entrance to the Ouvrage de Déramé. Note the defensive casemate on the left with two embrasures for machine guns and cannon. Ventilation slots were placed above the embrasures and a slot to drop grenades below. (Julie & Cedric Vaubourg, www.fortiffsere.fr)

longer distance with greater accuracy, enabling it to reach the centre of a fortress from a further distance, out of the range of the fortress' guns. Engineers compensated by building detached forts 3–4km from the centre. In 1885 the chemist Eugène Turpin patented the use of picric acid, a very powerful, but stable, explosive, in blasting charges. The French war ministry put it to military use as an explosive in artillery shells, renaming it 'melinite'. Its explosive power

'Torpedo-shell crisis', 1886								
Name	Construction date	Modernization date	Total cost (francs)	Men	Machine-gun turrets	75mm turrets	155mm turrets	Armoured observatories
23 – Charny	1887	1902–04	935,000	100	1			1
24 – Froideterre	1887	1902–05	1.1 million	125	2	1		2
25 – Thiaumont	1887	1902–05	410,000	100	1			1
26 – Hardaumont	1887	1904	900,000					
27 – La Laufée	1887	1904–06 1913–14	350,000	115		1		1
28 – Eix	1887	n/a						
29 – Déramé	1887	1902–07	1 million	150	1			1
30 – Fromeréville	1887	1900						
31 – Germonville	1887	n/a						
32 – Les Bruyères	1887	n/a						
33 – Bois-du-Chapitre	1888	n/a						
34 – Saint-Maure	1888	n/a						
35 – Baleycourt	1888	n/a						
36 – Manesel	1888	n/a						
37 – Châtillon	1888	n/a						
38 – Saint-Symphorien	1888	1900 1902	400,000	120				
39 – Jaulny	1889	n/a						
40 – Bezonvaux	1889	n/a						
41 – Maubois	1889	n/a						
42 – Josemont	1887	n/a						

was tremendous. Time-delayed fuses could keep the melinite from exploding until the shell had penetrated the earth covering the fort's masonry vaulting, causing severe damage. This was a huge blow to fortress engineers. Masonry was the primary building material used in all fortifications built to date and melinite could turn a fortress into a useless death trap. An immediate solution to this crisis was needed. The engineers needed to find new protective material and they turned to modern technology, ushering in a new age of concrete-and-steel fortifications.

Concrete is made by mixing Portland cement with sand, pebbles and water. It was invented in the mid-19th century. The cement compound is first mixed with water to form a mortar, which is then mixed with sand and pebbles to create a hardened, durable surface with significantly greater resistance to melinite projectiles than ordinary masonry.

Tests were conducted by the French Army between December 1886 and May 1887 using 155mm and 220mm shells fired at test structures made with various formulas and thicknesses of concrete. These tests resulted in the development of specifications to be used in new construction. Vaulted ceilings, outer partitions and footings were to be 2.5m thick. Outer walls exposed to enemy fire were to be 4–6m thick with a layer of earth on top for camouflage. Counterscarp walls were to be 5m in height and 2–2.5m thick. Concrete was classified in three types, depending on the degree of protection needed, based on the density of concrete to aggregate. The less aggregate material (i.e. stone and sand) added to the cement, the more dense and strong the concrete. The base mix from which all categories would start was $30cm^3$ of sand and $90cm^3$ of pebbles. Type 1 had 200kg per square metre of cement added; type 2 had 300kg per square metre and type 3 had 400kg per square metre. Type 3, the most dense, was referred to as 'special concrete', and became the standard type of concrete used.

Engineers now had to determine which of the existing masonry forts could be modified and which would have to be abandoned. Fortunately, tests showed that the engineers could modify the existing forts by adding a layer of concrete to the outer surface. The layer of earth covering the top of the masonry vaulting was removed to prepare a foundation for a new layer of concrete. A layer of compacted sand 1–1.5m thick was placed between the new concrete and the old masonry roof. In some cases the masonry vaulting was completely removed

Fort Marre, left bank. An excellent example of the modernization process. A layer of concrete was added over the original masonry façade. Openings were left in the original archways. Compare with the photograph of the barracks on p. 5. (Julie & Cedric Vaubourg, www.fortiffsere.fr)

and replaced with concrete, which was then covered with 50cm of earth for camouflage.

Barracks façades were reinforced using two different methods. The original façades were built with windows and doors open to the outside to allow light and air to reach the rooms inside. These windows and doors were contained within an archway that corresponded to the vaulted shape of the roof of the interior chambers. The first method of modification was to cover the façade completely with a layer of concrete, leaving a corridor between the new concrete layer and the old masonry façade. The second method was to build the concrete cover directly against the old masonry, leaving an opening for the original archway. The second method was used at Forts Douaumont, Vaux, Moulainville, Marre and Tavannes. Douaumont was the first of the original forts to be modernized, starting in 1887.

The engineers also modified the profile and flanking defences of the ditch surrounding the forts. The original profile included a wall on both the outer (counterscarp) and inner (escarp) walls on either side of the ditch. It also included casemates (called 'caponiers') that extended across the ditch to provide flanking fire down the angle of the ditch. Because of their increased velocity and reduced angle of fire, artillery shells could now strike and breach the face of the wall of the escarp and damage or destroy the caponiers. To fix this problem the escarp walls were removed and replaced with a spiked iron fence and the angle of the slope of the escarp leading up to the ramparts was decreased. Caponiers were replaced by casemates built into the outer wall of the counterscarp, concealed and invulnerable to direct enemy fire.

Reinforced concrete was introduced at Verdun in 1896 for roofs and walls most exposed to shellfire, such as the top of the counterscarp casemates and flanking casemates. These were known as 'Bourges casemates' after the French proving ground at Bourges. Special concrete was reinforced with 10mm-thick metal rods, placed in square groupings of 15cm, with each grouping 15–20cm apart. The metal density was either 85kg per cubic metre or 65kg depending on the degree of protection required. Reinforced concrete could withstand shelling from a 270mm gun. It was stronger than special concrete of the same thickness and presented a smaller profile. The thickness was a minimum of 1.2m for tunnels, and up to 1.8m for exposed surfaces. After additional artillery tests in 1912 the thickness was increased to 2.1m. After 1898 reinforced concrete was used in the modernization of existing forts and exclusively in the new forts. Fort Vacherauville and the Ouvrage

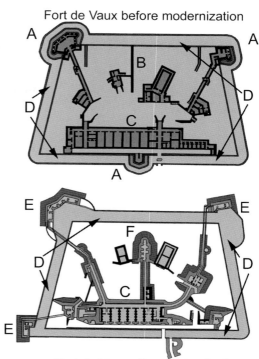

Fort de Vaux before modernization

Fort de Vaux after modernization

Fort Vaux was modernized between 1888 and 1912. The defensive caponiers (A) were converted to counterscarp casemates (E). The guns on the cavalier (B) were replaced with armoured turrets (F). The barracks (C) was reinforced with a layer of concrete. The centre of the fort was surrounded by a ditch (D). (Marcus Massing collection)

Final generation – all concrete								
Name	Construction date	Modernization date	Total cost (francs)	Men	Machine-gun turrets	75mm turrets	155mm turrets	Armoured observatories
43 – La Falouse	1906	n/a	550,000	80	1	1		2
44 – Vacherauville	1910	n/a	2.4 million	200	1	1	2	4

Entrance to the north-west casemate flanking the ditch of Fort Vaux. This casemate was attacked by German pioneers on 1 June 1916. After the casemate was captured, the Germans proceeded into tunnels that connected the casemate with the interior of the fort. A battle took place inside the tunnels until the fort surrendered on 7 June. (Author's collection)

de la Falouse were the last generation of fortifications to be built entirely in concrete at Verdun.

Another effect of the torpedo-shell crisis was the increased vulnerability of artillery pieces placed in open ramparts on the top of the forts. Beginning in 1887 the artillery pieces were removed from the ramparts and placed in flanking batteries between the forts. Approximately 32 external batteries were built between 1887 and 1894. The external gun batteries consisted of an entrenched access route leading to the gun platforms. There were typically four platforms separated by traverses 12m thick to defend them from enfilading fire. Defending infantry were shielded by masonry parapets. To the rear of each traverse were small personnel shelters with concrete roofs where soldiers could seek refuge from shrapnel fire. After the year 1900 modifications were made to the shelters, including thicker concrete to improve protection for the soldiers.

A more effective solution to the torpedo-shell crisis was the development of armour plating to protect the guns. The new high-explosive shells could fire shrapnel rounds onto artillery troops in open ramparts. A new material was required to shield both the gun and the gunner. The German firm Gruson conducted tests to find the best type of iron or steel, or a combination of both, that could withstand the effects of high-explosive shells. Gruson developed a series of rounded cast-iron armour plates that were connected together in a straight line to form an armoured casemate. Armour plating was first used around gun embrasures and as a shutter to protect the guns if the position

A TYPE GF4 TURRET FOR TWO HOTCHKISS MODEL 1900 MACHINE GUNS

This turret was a common armoured feature added to the forts after the torpedo-shell crisis of 1886. The turret was coupled with an armoured observation post (**1**). It was made of chrome steel and housed two machine guns. A painted panorama (**2**) ran along the inside ceiling to guide the observers if they could not see out of the viewing ports. The turret was the only part that revolved around a central piston (**3**). It was raised and lowered using a hand crank (**4**). The concrete cylinder housing the turret and lift mechanism was surrounded by an armoured collar for additional protection (**5**). The second floor and gun chamber were accessed by a ladder. The turret's weight was balanced by a counterweight (**6**) hung from chains (**7**) that ran on a wheel. Gas was removed by a hand ventilator (**8**). A gallery (**9**) led to the armoured observatory (**10**), accessed by a ladder. The observer could move the floor (**11**) up and down to adjust to his height. The two armoured elements were housed in special (**12**) and category 2 (**13**) concrete.

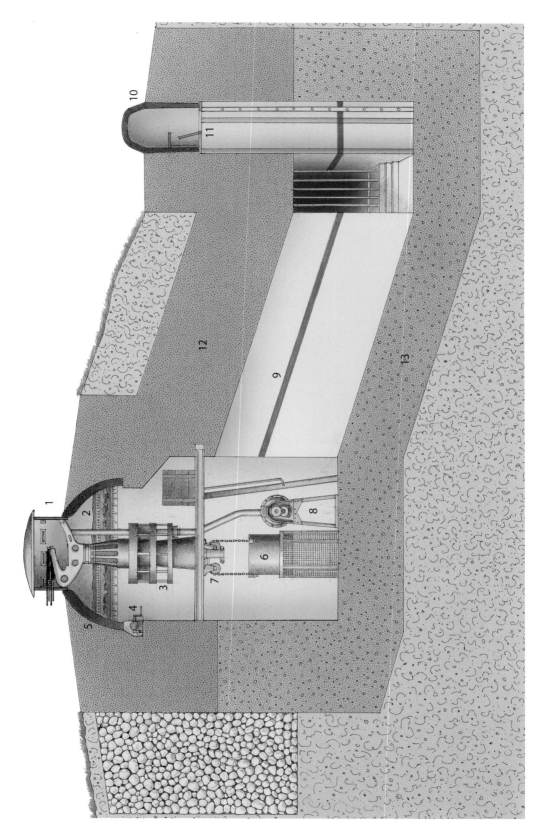

The Bussière turret for two 155mm guns. The only one of its kind installed at Verdun. It is located behind Fort Souville. (Author's collection)

was shelled. The first armoured gun turret was invented by the British Captain Cowper Coles and was mounted on British naval vessels starting in 1857. In Germany Hauptmann Maximilian Schumann developed a revolving turret for two 15cm guns for land-based fortifications. Commandant Mougin, a French engineer, designed a revolving turret for two 155mm cannon invented by Colonel Charles de Bange. The Mougin turret, like the Schumann model, was built by connecting curved steel plates to form a spherical cylinder that could revolve 360 degrees. The Mougin model was adopted for use in several early Séré de Rivières fortifications; however, none were installed at Verdun.

In 1888 the French conducted tests on three turret models at Chalons: a turret developed by the Montluçon firm, a Mougin turret and a third, designed by the French engineer Bussière, that not only revolved but could be raised and lowered to hide the guns below the surface. His design was built by Fives and Châtillon and used a hydraulic piston run by a steam engine to raise the turret to a height of 80cm. The tests revealed the efficacy of the eclipsable turret, and this was the model chosen by the French Army for their fortifications. A Bussière prototype was installed to the rear of Fort Souville; however, it was the only model of its type installed because the hydraulic mechanism frequently malfunctioned and it took too long to raise the turret.

In 1889 Commandant Galopin, also of the armoured service, created a

Galopin 155R turret, Fort Douaumont. The inside of a similar turret is shown on p. 41. (Author's collection)

similar turret for two Bange-model 155mm long-barrelled guns, with an improved engine that could raise and lower the guns in as little as three seconds and revolve the turret 360 degrees in six seconds. It had a superb weight balance, assisted by two 45-ton counterweights. The turret consisted of a cylindrical wall 45cm thick and 5.5m in diameter, covered by a spherical cap 30cm thick. This was far superior to the Bussière model and required only one man to raise and lower the turret. Each gun had a hydraulic brake to reduce its recoil

A 75mm gun turret coupled with an armoured observation post. Location unknown but most likely on the right bank. (National Archives of the US)

after firing. However, because of their large size and high price of 850,000 francs, only five of the two-gun Galopin turrets were built.

A cheaper model of the Galopin turret with a single 155mm R-model gun was chosen in 1907. The 'R' stood for *raccourci* – a shortened barrel with a length of 1.185m, as opposed to 3.015m for the larger model. It was built at the Châtillon-Commentry forge. The single-gun Galopin turret was remarkable. It was as powerful as its two-gun predecessor but smaller in diameter, with a thinner but stronger cylinder wall (30cm), weighed 72 tons and cost 400,000 francs. The range of the gun was 7,500m. Because of the reduced length of the barrel, the turret was smaller (4.1m diameter versus 5.5 for the larger model) and cheaper. The operating crew was 20–22 men. The first three Galopin 155R turrets were installed at Forts Douaumont, Moulainville and Rozelier in 1908. Two others were installed in 1911 at Fort Vacherauville.

Galopin also designed a turret for two rapid-fire 75mm guns with shortened barrels. Built by the firm Saint-Jacques de Montluçon, this turret was adopted for use in 1901. It could fire 20–22 rounds per minute at a velocity of 441m per second, with a range of 4,875m for shrapnel shells and 4,680m for explosive shells. It used the same munitions as the 75mm field gun. The gun chamber rested on a cylindrical piston that could rotate 360 degrees and be raised and lowered for firing. The turret was 2.3m in diameter and the protective cap was 30cm thick. A hand-operated crank was used to raise and lower the 85-ton turret, assisted and balanced by a counterweight. The turret had two levels; the gun chamber was on the upper level and on the lower level the turret was raised, lowered and turned and supplied with munitions hoisted up to the gun chamber using a manually operated lift. The guns were mounted on a special carriage with a maximum depression and elevation of -7 and +12.45 degrees respectively. The entire turret piece was housed inside a concrete cylinder. The collar surrounding the turret cylinder was originally made of concrete but tests conducted in 1912 using a 280mm gun cracked the concrete and dislodged the turret. The concrete collar was replaced by one made of moulded steel, and 14 of these turrets were in place at Verdun by 1914. Their cost was 310,000 francs each.

The French also used machine guns for defence against enemy infantry attack. In July 1893, Army engineers began to work on a turret model for the machine gun. The final model used, the GF4 Model 1899, was built by

Machine-gun turret and armoured observation post, Fort Douaumont. The two Hotchkiss machine-gun barrels protruded from the oval embrasures on the right side. Slits allowed the gunner to see outside. The turret revolved 360 degrees and could be raised for firing and lowered for protection from incoming shells. (Author's collection)

Châtillon-Commentry. It housed twin Hotchkiss 8mm machine guns. The two guns were placed on a special carriage, with one gun above the other so that one could fire while the other cooled down. The range of the guns was 2,400m and they could fire 600 rounds per minute. The gun barrels protruded from the turret cylinder wall during firing and the carriage was built so the barrels could be pulled back inside the turret when it was lowered. This allowed the diameter of the turret to be reduced to 1.31m. The turret cap was 12cm thick. The walls were made of 20cm-thick chrome steel and the mechanism could be raised to 83cm. It was raised only at the moment of assault and could withstand small-arms fire. The gun chamber rested on a pivoting column. The turret column was raised and lowered manually with the help of a counterweight. The gunner used his legs to revolve the turret. Each turret had a four-man crew. The turret weighed 25 tons and cost 72,000 francs. A total of 29 machine-gun turrets were installed at Verdun between 1895 and 1914.

It was important to shield or protect the fort's artillery observers to the same degree as the guns. The first armoured observation posts appeared in 1892. The observatory was in the shape of a bell. It was a single piece of steel 20cm thick with a spherical top. Three small viewing ports gave the observer a viewing angle of 240 degrees. Each observatory was coupled with a gun turret and the two were connected by an acoustic communications tube. The gunner could raise and lower the floor to adjust it to his height. The observation post was reached by a ladder from the gallery below. It weighed 7.5 tons and cost 15,000 francs. It could hold one observer and was oriented to allow observation of the front. The French observatories did not

B   A BOURGES CASEMATE FOR TWO 75MM CANNON – FORT VAUX

Bourges casemates were added to provide flanking protection to the intervals between the forts. This plate is representative of most Bourges casemates. It includes: (**1**) the tunnel entry from the barracks area of the fort; (**2**) gun chambers for 75mm cannon; (**3**) gun embrasures with steel shutters to block off the embrasures in case of shelling or attack; (**4**) a staircase leading to the lower level where the munitions were stored; (**5**) a passage through to the lower floor – munitions were passed by hand from the lower to the upper level; (**6**) a short ladder leading to the observatory platform; (**7**) the observation window; (**8**) a wall built to block enfilading fire from the forward area; (**9**) the escarpment wall with the ditch below.

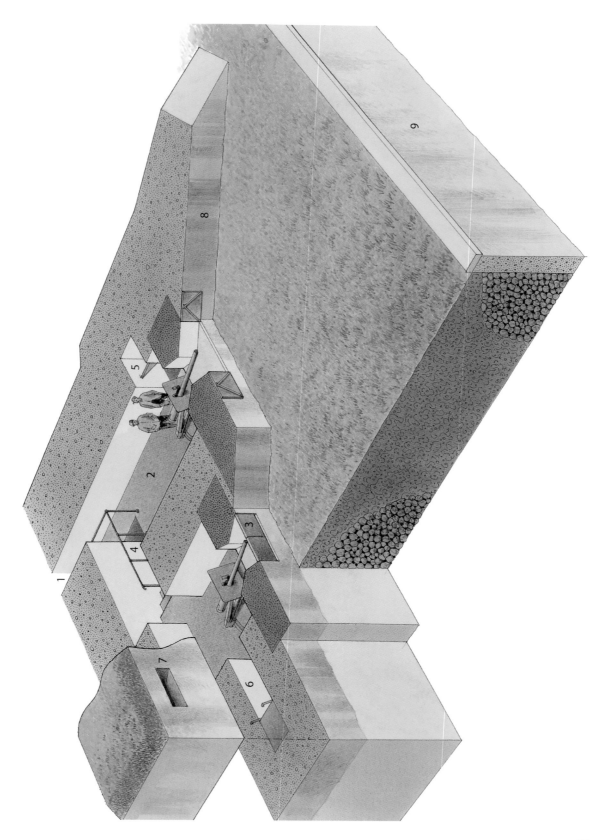

21

have the capability to hold more sophisticated optical equipment like the German-built models did. In 1905 a new model was developed with a diameter 20cm larger than the original (52cm). Observatories served two functions: for surveillance of the battlefield and for directing artillery fire. The observatories were built by Creusot; 47 were installed at Verdun.

Beginning in 1905 each fort was equipped with armoured sentry posts for infantry observation. These were smaller than the artillery posts, with 5cm of armour, designed to protect sentries from shrapnel fire. They were also equipped with three viewing ports. There were two models: one built into the parapet with an armoured entry door in the rear, and the other model was built above a rampart shelter, accessible by ladder. There were typically two posts to watch the rear of the fort.

Combat shelters were built into the rear of the trench line to protect the forward infantry during enemy bombardment. The shelters were hidden from view on the counterslope of the hill. There were two sizes – the smaller could accommodate half an infantry company, and the larger could accommodate a whole company. It was the job of these men to man the forward trenches in their area. There were two models – 1898 and 1913 – but at Verdun only the 1898 model was built. The 1898 model sheltered a full company in four bomb-proof chambers 4m by 10m in size perpendicular to the façade (a shelter for a half company had two chambers). They were covered by 1.6m of concrete and 20cm of earth. The walls were 2m thick and the façade was built of masonry masked with a concrete façade 1.2m wide, with a corridor running behind it leading to each chamber. The shelters included latrines and a cistern in the cellar to store fresh water. Kitchens were later added to make the shelter self-sustaining. The shelters were designated according to the two works on their flanks. For example, the shelters between Forts Douaumont and Vaux were designated DV-1, DV-2, etc. There were a total of 34 combat shelters built at Verdun.

In 1889 French engineers built four *abris cavernes* – 'cavern shelters' – which were personnel shelters dug into the hillside. The most famous of these is the Four Chimneys Shelter near the Froideterre Works. Two separate but parallel entrances were dug into the hillside and a set of stairs led from each entrance down a 16m-long tunnel to a large vaulted chamber 3.5m wide by

70m long running perpendicular to the entrance tunnels. The cavern shelter was built 7.5m below the surface. Each shelter could accommodate 125 soldiers (approximately half a company), and each had four ventilation stacks. Three other cavern shelters were built near Douaumont (Abri 320), behind Fort Souville and at Sartelles-Chana, which had a 100m-long chamber.

The final addition to the fortress defences was a Bourges casemate for 75mm cannon. They were made entirely of concrete. The ceiling and the masking walls were made of reinforced concrete, and the rest was made of special concrete. Their profile gave the appearance of steps with a forward and rear echelon. They had one or two firing chambers, one in each echelon, the forward chamber protected by a long wall and the rear chamber by the wall of the forward chamber. They were encased in the slope of the ramparts on the flanks of the forts. Each had two levels. The upper level contained the gun chambers and the lower level the munitions and a small crew quarters. Most Bourges casemates were connected by tunnel to the main part of the fort.

The Bourges casemates housed 75mm field guns on special carriages that pivoted on the centre of each embrasure, the rear of the carriage sliding along a groove in the floor. The horizontal field of fire was 60 degrees and the vertical firing angles ranged from -10 to +15 degrees. The maximum range of the gun was 5,600m. Each gun was supplied with 500 shells, which were stored in the lower level and lifted by hand to the gun level through an opening in the floor next to each piece. A hoist was attached to a rail that ran along the ceiling to change damaged gun barrels. Each casemate had a 16-man crew. The first Bourges casemate was installed at Fort Haudainville, and equipped with two 95mm model 1888 guns that could fire five rounds per minute.

The old Vauban citadel remained an integral part of Verdun's defences. Bomb-proof shelters underneath the citadel provided a refuge for thousands of soldiers throughout the battle. Between 1890 and 1894, 2,300m of tunnels 4–6m wide and 1,700m of tunnels 2.5m wide were dug 16m below the rock of the citadel. The tunnel system included lodging for 2,000 soldiers with water, telephones, infirmaries and kitchens.

From 1874 to 1914 France had spent 820 million francs on the Verdun fortress, 206 million of this from 1900 to 1914 (in 1913, 3 francs was equal to 1 euro as of 2007). With 28 forts and principal fortified works, Verdun was the most modern fortification system in France. As war approached, the finishing touches were being made to Fort Vacherauville, and it lacked only its machine-gun turret. Two turrets awaited installation at Douaumont and Bois-Bourrus.

Ditch and entrance to Fort Sartelles, left bank. The entrance was placed in the ditch and defended by a double caponier (seen in the foreground). (Author's collection)

TOUR OF THE SITE

Verdun was surrounded by two rings of fortifications, artillery batteries and shelters. The outer ring was 45km in circumference, and the inner ring 25km. In the centre was the 17th-century Vauban fortress with its bastioned walls, ornate gateways and citadel. The river Meuse flows from south to north through Verdun, dividing the fortress into two halves. Rolling hills rise to the east and west of the river. Deep, wooded ravines cut through the heights of the right bank. The slopes on the left bank are more gradual. The major forts were built on the most prominent points.

The forts were polygonal in shape. Each fort was unique, tailored to fit its location and mission. The forts differed in size from 182m by 140m (Regret) to 225m by 155m (Belrupt) to 400m by 300m (Douaumont – the largest). Each fort sat on the crest of a hill. The glacis sloped gently away from the centre in all directions, and it was covered with a broad belt of barbed wire mounted on posts, forming an impenetrable anti-personnel obstacle. It sloped gently uphill towards the fort until it reached the second obstacle, a ditch 5m deep and 10m wide. The outer wall of the ditch was called the counterscarp. Across the ditch from the counterscarp was the escarp, a gentle slope that rose up to the ramparts in the centre of the fort. The slope of the escarp was also covered by a belt of barbed wire.

Casemates were built into each corner, or salient angle, of the counterscarp wall to provide flanking fire down the entire angle of the ditch. Counterscarp casemates were simple in design, built of special concrete with walls 2m thick

---

C   **THE ENTRY GATE AT FORT ROZELIER**

One of the more ornate entry gates of the Verdun forts. The main road (**1**) leads to the original entry. The ramp (**2**) leads to the wartime entry (**3**) in the ditch (**4**). The walls of the wartime entry were painted white with a red stripe to denote this area as bomb-proof. The armoured door leads to the wartime concrete barracks. At the top is a sentry post (**5**), which defends

access to a bridge and drawbridge (**6**). Additional defences inside the portal include a rolling bridge (**7**) and rifle embrasures (**8**). The rear of the entry is protected by an armoured door (**9**). Offices for NCOs are located to the right (**10**). The entry portal (**11**) reveals the ornate design of many of the Verdun forts.

25

Fort Dugny. This is a tunnel leading to the double casemate defending the ditch at the front of the fort. The red stripes denote this tunnel as being bomb-proof. (Author's collection)

on the sides and rear, and a 1.5m-thick façade wall. They also had a defensive ditch running along the front that was 2–3m wide and 4m deep. The casemate gun chambers were 4.5m long and 9m wide and contained two guns in embrasures 2.5m apart. Vents were placed above each embrasure to allow fumes from the guns to escape. Below each embrasure was a small slot with a trapdoor. If the enemy was attacking the casemate embrasure, defenders could drop grenades into the ditch through the slot. Each casemate had a latrine, a sleeping area, munitions storage rooms, and an opening in the outer wall for an oxygen- or acetylene-powered projector to illuminate the ditch at night.

The casemate was connected to the centre of the fort by a tunnel, accessed by a staircase, leading to the central part of the fort. An armoured door blocked the entry to the casemate from the tunnel. A second staircase at the other end of the tunnel led up into the centre of the fort. The main elements of the fort were connected by additional underground tunnels that were 1–2.5m wide with vaulted roofs. Entrances to the tunnels were barred by steel gates and armoured doors equipped with rifle embrasures.

The ramparts were located at the top of the fort, beyond the escarp, in the central redoubt of the fort. In the earlier forts, before armoured turrets were used, field-artillery pieces were placed on this rampart on gun platforms separated by banks of earth called traverses, which gave additional protection to the gun on the flanks. Shelters or gun-storage garages were built under the traverses. Infantry parapets were also built to defend against an infantry attack on the fort. From the parapets defenders could see and fire upon infantry approaching the fort. Each fort had picket shelters under the central part of the fort where troops waited to man the infantry parapets. Exits led from the shelters to the ramparts on top.

When armoured turrets for the cannon were installed after 1886, they were placed in the centre of the former ramparts. The armoured machine-gun turrets were typically placed in the front corners. Each turret was coupled with a steel observation post located a few metres away. The Bourges casemates were placed on each flank of the rampart at the rear of the fort and their gun embrasures faced towards the two intervals.

The ditch surrounded the entire fort, including the rear, the part of the fort referred to as the 'gorge'. The living quarters for the men and the entrance to the fort was located at the gorge. The entrance to the fort was located across the ditch. In the earlier forts a bridge was constructed across the ditch to the entrance portal. Two-thirds of the way across the ditch the bridge was cut and the second part formed a drawbridge that could be raised up against the face of the entry gate. Some forts had a small blockhouse at the top of the ditch across from the gorge with a small casemate with rifle embrasures to guard the access road leading to the fort.

The first obstacle after the drawbridge was an iron gate. A second obstacle called a rolling bridge was located on the other side of the gate. This was a small wooden bridge on a steel frame that could be rolled back into a slot in the side of the passageway to reveal a pit underneath. An armoured door

with rifle embrasures provided further protection after passing over the rolling bridge. The area between the gate and the armoured door was called the vestibule and it was pierced on both sides with *meurtrières* (rifle embrasures) to defend the entryway. Beyond the entryway was a central corridor that led to the heart of the fort – a central courtyard or tunnels that led to other parts of the fort.

After the torpedo-shell crisis the engineers added a second 'wartime' entry in the base of the ditch. In some forts where the original entrance was not built at the base of the ditch, there was both a peacetime entry above (with a bridge obstacle) and a wartime entry below. The wartime entry also had defensive features including a bridge over a small ditch, a rolling bridge and rifle embrasures. It guarded the access to bomb-proof concrete barracks built after the torpedo-shell crisis, located below the original barracks. The walls in the wartime barracks and tunnels were painted white with a horizontal red stripe running parallel to the floor halfway up the wall to indicate they were bomb-proof. The barracks were on one or two levels and included quarters for the men and officers, kitchens, latrines, an infirmary and storage for provisions. The living quarters consisted of vaulted chambers (also referred to in French reports as 'casemates') that were 6m wide and 15m long, with a door leading to a corridor 2–2.5m wide that ran along the rear of the barracks. Kitchens were located on the ground floor of the barracks, with the same dimensions as the living quarters. The kitchen area was split by a partition wall into two areas. The cooking and food-preparation area was located in the part of the chamber with an opening to the outside so it would be well lit, while the food was stored in the darker, cooler area at the back. Latrines were located on the flanks of the barracks. Below each latrine was a well of $1m^3$, which was always as well ventilated as possible.

Powder magazines were located deep inside the fort, as far as possible from the barracks. Each magazine was built to store 100 tons of powder in vaulted chambers 6–8m wide. Infantry munitions magazines also stocked bullets

Vestibule inside the entrance gate of Fort Dugny. It is defended by triple-armoured doors. The central gallery is behind the doors and leads to two exits to the right and left at the end of the corridor. The tunnels halfway down branch off to barracks rooms and defensive casemates to the right and left. (Author's collection)

A view from Fort Vaux across the Woevre Plain in the direction of Abaucourt. This shows the excellent vantage point of the forts. (National Archives of the US)

for the infantry, and could hold up to 300,000 rounds. To prevent an explosion caused by a fire or spark, open flames were not permitted inside the magazine. Instead, lamps were placed in niches at the end of the chamber behind heavy glass panels, accessible from a corridor outside the magazine. To prevent sparks, no metal of any kind except brass was permitted. A double-layered floor of oak was built 40cm above the masonry floor to prevent spoilage of powder from humidity. Ventilation conduits allowed the air to circulate freely inside the chamber, keeping dampness to a minimum.

The barracks of Fort Vaux showing modifications and repairs made to the façade. The concrete was added to the façade and roof of the barracks during the modernization of 1888–95. (National Archives of the US)

PRINCIPLES OF DEFENCE

The Treaty of Frankfurt resulted in France's loss of the province of Alsace and part of Lorraine to Germany. In 1871 the Germans began construction of the powerful Moselstellung (Moselle Position) at Metz, just 60km from Verdun. France had now lost its strong fortresses of Metz and Strasbourg, leaving the entire Woevre Plain and the road to Paris undefended. France quickly assembled a commission to design a new defensive system. Verdun traditionally guarded the eastern border and important lines of communication from north to south and east to west. Verdun's mission, with its new ring of forts, was to hold the Meuse position, cover the concentration of the field army, inhibit enemy freedom of manoeuvre and interdict the Metz–Paris road and railway line. Verdun was directly in the path and the first objective of a German advance from Metz. With its ring of forts it also served as a strong assembly point for French forces, giving it an added offensive role.

On the right bank of the Meuse it was necessary to defend both the river valley and the wide, flat Woevre Plain to the east from enemy attack. The heights of the right bank consisted of wooded ravines and defiles – very difficult terrain on which to manoeuvre a large army. The fortress never stopped evolving from 1874 to 1914. When World War I broke out the main fortress line was buttressed on the north by Fort Douaumont on Hill 396, which covered the northern approaches, and on the south at Fort Rozelier on Hill 39, which covered the road to Metz. Between these two positions was the Bois-Brule, where Fort Tavannes would guard the Paris–Metz railway line and the Verdun–Etain–Metz road. The south side of the Metz road and the upstream direction (south of Verdun) of the Meuse was guarded by strong positions at Saint-Symphorien and Haudainville. The downstream direction (north of Verdun) of the right bank would be guarded by a small infantry fort at Froideterre.

On the left bank the land was less rugged than the right bank, with the highest hills less than 300m in height. The Paris–Metz road and railway continued through the heart of the left-bank forts. Fort Bois Bourrus would be the strongpoint of the left bank, covered on the left by Fort Landrecourt. Fort Dugny crossed fire with Fort Haudainville. The downstream direction was guarded by the powerful Fort Vacherauville. The Charny infantry works crossed fire with Froideterre.

Verdun was considered a ring fort, defending a retrenched camp, a large fortified area with several lines of defence. The main mission of the fortress was to interdict the passage of an army or to keep the enemy out of range of the central position. In earlier times the central position was the town or city defended by a citadel. The Verdun ring was not defending its citadel, as this had no significant military value, and, standing alone, it was considered a 'nesting place for enemy shells' and a death trap for a besieged army. Rather, it was built to prevent the enemy from using its roads and railways to reach the interior of France. Most of Europe had given up the bastioned trace fortification design, including Général Séré de Rivières. He had settled on a polygonal shape for simplicity of form. The polygon had two distinct advantages: it adapted well to irregular terrain (such as Verdun), and, being smaller in size, it needed less masonry to build, had a reduced perimeter and required fewer men and arms to defend. The forts were intentionally built to be weaker in the rear so that, in case of capture, batteries to the rear could fire on the weaker gorge of the fort, inflicting significant damage to the barracks, making it untenable to an enemy. This was known as the principle of irreversibility.

Detached forts, such as those at Verdun, were located where they could keep the enemy guns out of range of the centre of the fortress. The forts were placed to be within range of each other. This is the principle of mutual support, where each fort could fire on another if enemy troops reached the top of the fort. The forts were also placed where they could adequately cover the interval between themselves. In some cases it was necessary to add interval batteries to augment the firepower of the fort's guns. Intermediate infantry works, small infantry forts, were added to provide additional protection and coverage between the main forts. They were surrounded by a ditch and equipped with Bourges casemates and machine-gun turrets (La Laufée and Froideterre were each equipped with a 75mm turret). The intermediate infantry works provided cover for dead zones between the major forts. They were also built to protect their defenders from enemy bombardment and to resist an enemy infantry attack.

The main element of the fortress of Verdun was the 'fort'. It served initially as a large artillery battery defended by infantry. After the torpedo-shell crisis the rampart cannon of the forts were dispersed into multiple annex batteries

Fort Moulainville. The entrance and barracks is to the left. The Bourges casemate, 75mm gun turret and armoured observation post is to the right. (National Archives of the US)

that were harder for the enemy to locate. Mixed in with these batteries were combat shelters and intermediate infantry works. Finally, munitions stocks were dispersed into decentralized magazines. The post-1886 forts became observation posts tasked with flanking the intervals between the forts. Machine guns in turrets and 75mm guns defended the approaches to the forts. Some of the forts retained their rampart guns, of 80mm and 90mm calibre, for the same function. Larger-calibre 155mm guns for long-range interdiction of enemy troops were placed in turrets. The forts were built

to withstand bombardment from the new high-explosive shells. They included obstacles (ditches, walls, barbed wire, etc.) to enable them to withstand an infantry attack. They provided shelter for defenders and protection for artillery up to the time they were needed. Their defensive weapons had adequate range to keep enemy infantry at bay and they provided flanking fire to cover any interval position that came under attack.

Double casemate defending the ditch in the north-west corner of Fort Douaumont. It is remarkably well preserved despite the heavy bombardment it suffered. Note the remains of the counterscarp wall on the left edge of the photograph. (Author's collection)

The forts of 1874 consisted of a rampart made of earth preceded by a ditch. The ditch required defensive armaments to keep an enemy from crossing over it to the centre of the fort. Flanking guns were placed in casemates at the end of each angle of the ditch to cover that particular angle. Each was under surveillance from the casemate.

Counterscarp casemates were completely masked from enemy view and enfiladed the ditch from the reverse. Their drawback is they were vulnerable to mining from outside the fort. Access tunnels running under the ditch could be cut off from the centre of the fort. The goal of an attacker was to cross the ditch using a number of methods: dropping ladders into the ditch; using a siege bridge to cross over the ditch; or by regular attack, by destroying the counterscarp with artillery then blasting a breach in the escarp. Therefore the ditch was built as wide and deep as possible to keep the enemy under flanking fire as long as possible.

Artillery was essential to the defence of the fortified area. For the best protection possible it was placed inside the perimeter of the forts, originally on ramparts and later in armoured turrets. Many field guns were placed in annex batteries outside the forts to cover the places that could not be adequately covered by the fort's guns. Field-artillery pieces were being replaced at a fast pace by armoured turrets, and were dispersed from within

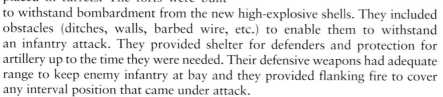

D NEXT PAGE: FORT DUGNY, LEFT BANK, VERDUN

Fort Dugny is one of the original redoubts and Panic Forts. It was modernized between 1901 and 1908. The components of the fort are as follows: (**1**) entry ramp from the rear; (**2**) entry gate with sentry post to the right that passes between the barbed-wire-covered glacis (**3**); (**4**) the gorge front; (**5**) entry gate; (**6**) casemates defending the gorge front with a small ditch along the face of the casemate and the façade of the barracks (**7**); (**8**) Bourges casemate; (**9**) covered way leading to infantry exits from the back of the barracks – both on the right and left sides; (**10**) traverse shelters; (**11**) infantry parapets with armoured sentry post; (**12**) machine-gun turrets; (**13**) entrance to the machine-gun turrets – right and left; (**14**) entrance to the tunnel leading to the double casemate in the centre; (**15**) 75mm turret; (**16**) armoured artillery observation post; (**17** and **19**) simple ditch casemates; (**18**) double casemate; (**20**) escarp; (**21**) counterscarp wall; (**22**) ditch.

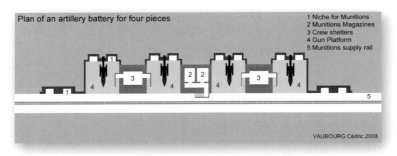

Plan of an interval artillery battery for four cannon. Munitions and personnel shelters were placed in the traverses between the gun platforms. (Julie & Cedric Vaubourg, www.fortiffsere.fr)

Plan of an artillery battery for four pieces

1 Niche for Munitions
2 Munitions Magazines
3 Crew shelters
4 Gun Platform
5 Munitions supply rail

VAUBOURG Cédric 2008

the forts to interval batteries defended by a line of infantry trenches with combat shelters. This zone, as it thickened with more and more elements, became an integral part of the principal line, and it became important for the main fort to be able to defend this interval zone. Beginning in 1885, flanking Bourges casemates were added to the flanks of each fort to defend the intervals between the forts. There were a number of artillery emplacements outside the forts. Protective batteries were designed to defend the infantry in the outer line of defence. They consisted of two types. The first were the 'Crest batteries', which were used for direct fire to slow down the enemy; they were in view of the enemy on the crest of the hill and protected behind ramparts. The second type was hidden from view behind the crest and was used for indirect fire against defiladed positions. Infantry positions were placed to slow down the attacking enemy infantry and to defend the batteries placed outside the forts. These positions were built when and where they were needed. After 1900 the Army adopted the concept of creating permanent positions in the intervals. These would be built out of concrete and provide shelter for a company or half-company of troops.

The fortress of Verdun was laid out as follows, from the outer perimeter to the central point or 'node' of the fortified area (in the case of Verdun, the old citadel was the centre):

The main line of resistance was located approximately 3km in advance of the principal line of defence and consisted of trenches and fieldworks built in peacetime using natural obstacles and entrenchments. It was prepared in advance to allow for quick occupation in time of emergency. At Verdun this was the forward trench line at the base of the hills, under cover of the guns in the principal line of defence on the heights above.

The principal line of defence included the detached forts, external gun batteries, interval infantry works and combat shelters. The fortifications of the principal line of defence were the key to the defences and the enemy would be compelled to attack them.

The centre point (node) provided a safe location for the commanders and the supplies needed to maintain the system of fortifications.

With the arrival of the torpedo-shell crisis in 1886, this concept was necessarily modified. The original concepts for the outer line and the principal line of defence were kept intact, but a new 'line of sustainment' was added a few kilometres behind the principal line of defence in order to prevent a breakthrough if the outer line fell, which is what happened at Verdun in 1916. The line of sustainment was 2–3km to the rear of the principal line of defence and crossed fire at each end with a fort on the principal line. It consisted of strong positions with external batteries and infantry defences. The line included the older forts built on the heights above Verdun as well as some fieldworks built as war approached.

Due to the quantity of munitions needed for all of the guns it would have been too expensive to build enough magazines inside the forts. It would also have been too dangerous to concentrate all the munitions for a sector in one place, as they could be captured or destroyed. Therefore, a munitions storage system was created. In each fort or position, a small stock was kept in a bomb-proof magazine. This included a stock of powder for the projectile (for ordinary shells and high explosive), plus fuses, detonators and infantry munitions. In each interval or annex battery, a small quantity of shells (already prepared for the guns) were placed in a niche next to each piece. Small magazines to the rear of each battery held a one- or two-day supply. Intermediate magazines were larger and held enough stocks for several of the forward positions. They served as a central point between the sector magazines and the gun batteries and provided storage for ordinary and high-explosive shells, fuses and detonators, as well as a workshop to assemble the shells for delivery to the guns. Sector magazines supplied munitions for the entire sector. It held a one- or two-day supply of all types of shells and powder, fuses and detonators, and workshops for assembly.

All of these elements were connected by strategic roads. A 60cm-gauge railway carried munitions and supplies to the forward lines. There were two types of communication line – a peripheral route that followed the perimeter of the principal line of defence and branched off to the main forts and works, and a second system that connected the works to the centre point and branched off in all directions, like the spokes of a wheel.

The Army used telegraph wire to relay messages, but the lines were not connected to the forts. If a fort was encircled the wire could be cut, restricting the ability of the fort to communicate and coordinate a defence with the command. It could also create a psychological disadvantage for the defenders, giving them the feeling of being isolated. Therefore, the optical telegraph was used for communication between the forts. It was based on light signals from a lantern used to flash Morse code to other locations within view of the optical post. This new system was used in the forts and a network was developed to connect the forts by a grid throughout the north-eastern sector. Verdun itself was a key component of the optical-communications system.

THE LIVING SITE

The fortress of Verdun was garrisoned with infantry regiments, fortress troops, artillery crews and various specialists (engineers, mechanics, cooks, etc.). These men came from the surrounding regions of France, and many served in reserve regiments that trained at Verdun. After the war started, the men served and stayed with their unit unless allowed to go home on leave. Until the bombardment of Verdun began and it was no longer safe to remain in them, 70,000 soldiers lived in large barracks compounds located behind the main line of defence (at Marceau, Chevert, Jardin-Fontaine and Glorieux, to name a few). They were then moved to shelters or to one of the forts if their regiment was assigned to defend it. The central barracks were walled compounds with large multi-storied buildings equipped with kitchens, sleeping quarters, offices and recreational facilities. They were located on the outskirts of Verdun.

Barracks chambers of the Ouvrage de Dérame. Compare with the photograph at the top of p. 37, which shows the original bunks. Personal gear and rifles were stored out in the hallway. (Julie & Cedric Vaubourg, www.fortiffsere.fr)

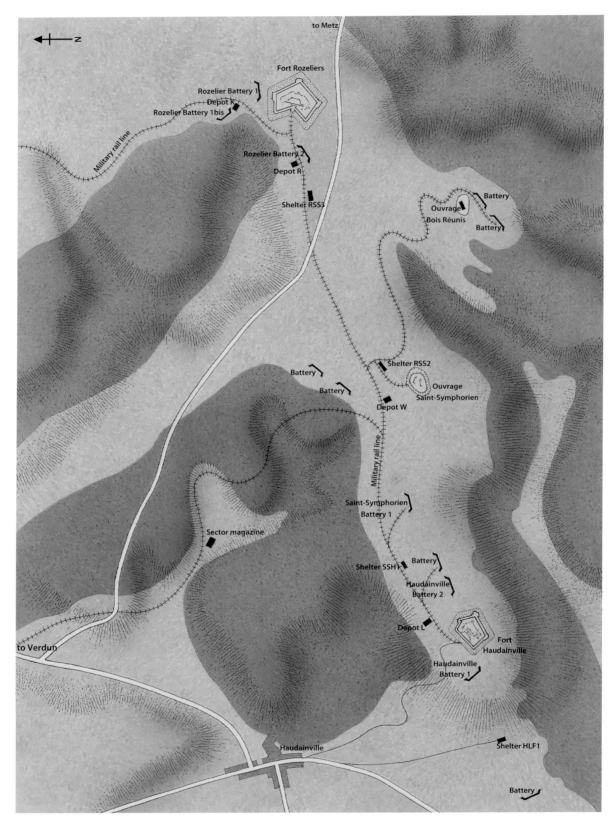

to Metz

Fort Rozeliers

Rozelier Battery 1
Depot K
Rozelier Battery 1bis

Military rail line

Rozelier Battery 2
Depot R

Shelter RSS3

Ouvrage
Bois Réunis

Battery

Battery

Shelter RSS2

Battery

Ouvrage
Saint-Symphorien

Battery

Depot W

Military rail line

Saint-Symphorien
Battery 1

Sector magazine

Shelter SSH1

Battery

Haudainville
Battery 2

Depot L

Fort
Haudainville

to Verdun

Haudainville
Battery 1

Haudainville

Shelter HLF1

Battery

Appearance of a restored chamber for troops at Fort d'Uxegney. Two men slept on each level. Their personal gear was stored on racks between the beds and at the foot of the bed. Each man had a three-legged stool. (Julie & Cedric Vaubourg, www.fortiffsere.fr)

The garrison at Verdun provided the forts with infantry and artillery troops. In pre-war times, reserve or regular units were rotated in and out of the forts in shifts. Each shift lasted one week and the forts were officially turned over from one unit to the next. As part of the turnover process between units, the highest-ranking officer of the relieving troops received, from the highest-ranking officer in charge of the unit being relieved, the keys to the fort, orders for the period of the rotation and an inventory of ammunition, water and food stocks (water was measured by the level of water in the fort's cistern). Other officers would take inventory of the stocks before the receipt was signed. Once all responsibility was transferred they were relieved.

The restored kitchen and stove at Fort d'Uxegney at Épinal. This fort, in the style of the Verdun forts, has been magnificently restored. (Julie & Cedric Vaubourg, www.fortiffsere.fr)

The relieving troops assumed guard duty while the rest of the soldiers took quarters in the barracks. In general, duty in the fort was dull and repetitious, consisting mostly of guard duty, practice drills with the artillery and weapons and maintenance of the fort to keep it in good condition. Keeping a fort in combat condition was a time-intensive job. Maintenance tasks included waterproofing the buildings to prevent damage from moisture and humidity, repairing leaks and flooding to underground rooms and tunnels, repairing damage to the masonry and concrete structures, removing overgrowth and cutting the grass to maintain an orderly

E THE SOUTH-EAST CORNER OF THE FORTRESS OF VERDUN

This sector includes two large forts, Haudainville and Rozelier. Between the two forts are the intermediate infantry works of Saint-Symphorien and Bois Réunis. Fort Haudainville was flanked by the Ouvrage de la Falouse, which was across the river Meuse. Fort Rozelier is actually flanked by the Ouvrage de Maubois; however, Déramé was a more powerful infantry work. Fort Rozelier guarded the Paris–Metz road and Fort Haudainville the approaches to Verdun from the south along the Meuse.

appearance and maintain fields of fire. Soldiers were also assigned tasks to clean the fort, work in the kitchen and maintain the fort's guns and their own personal equipment. If the fort was being modernized or repaired then the troops also assisted in the construction. Since each fort had police and jail cells it is logical to assume the commanders handled minor disciplinary problems inside the fort.

During their tour in the forts, the officers, enlisted men and non-commissioned officers (NCOs) were housed in the barracks chambers. The NCOs slept in the same rooms as the men while the officers were placed in a separate wing of the barracks. Barracks rooms typically housed 60 men per room (14 beds that slept four enlisted men each and two beds for four NCOs). Each officer was given 6m^2 of living space and a private cubicle. The commander had a single room close to his office and the telegraph station.

Each man was provided with his own sleeping space, composed of wooden planks laid on top of a wrought-iron bed frame with two levels, which could sleep four men, with two on each level (see photograph on p. 37). Each man's sleeping space was 2m long and 1.5m wide, separated by an interval of 74cm. The beds were connected to the wall and could be disassembled if the room needed to be used for other purposes, such as a magazine or assembly area. A wooden shelf and gun rack was located at the foot of each bed for the soldier's gear and rifle. A shelf for additional gear and private belongings was attached to the wall between each set of beds. Each man was supplied with a three-legged stool. The NCOs slept in single bunks of the same design. After 1885 a new type of bunk system was placed in the new forts that slept three men on each level. The bunks were connected together in one ensemble and the soldier's personal storage shelves and racks were sometimes located in a hallway outside the chamber (see photograph on p. 35).

The barracks chambers were heated by coal stoves of several different models (Choubersky, Joly, Vaillant, etc.). The stoves were placed in a niche in the wall midway along the chamber. The smoke escaped through a vent pipe connected to a chimney inside the wall between the chambers. Officers' rooms were heated by a stove placed in the centre with an exhaust pipe leading up to a vent in the ceiling. The barracks also contained an infirmary, usually in the same wing as the officers' quarters. The infirmary had storage space for medicine and medical equipment.

In wartime the windows to the outside were sealed with armoured rails, plunging the rooms into darkness. Lighting for the interior was provided by candles or oil lamps. Each chamber had a hanging lantern with an oil burner that hung from the vaulted ceiling. The fort also had a supply of portable lamps similar to those used by railway men. These portable lamps, as well as candles, oil and matches were stored in the main magazine in a 'lampisterie'.

Each fort had a cook who was assisted by men from the garrison. The men ate their meals in their chambers. Officers had a mess area with tables for dining. Food was prepared on coal-heated iron stoves built by the Vaillant company. Coal for the stove was stored in bins in one of the magazines. The stove was placed against the wall and a vent pipe ran up the wall into a conduit that led outside the barracks. There was also a large boiler for hot water and soup manufactured by the Bernard company that could hold 75 litres of liquid. A six-month supply of food was stored in the fort. Food stocks included: flour in 80kg sacks; biscuits in 50kg cases; rice in 60kg sacks; dried beans, peas, and lentils in 80kg sacks; coffee; salt in 60kg sacks;

and refined sugar in 185kg cases. In addition there was a supply of salted meats, barrels of lard, wine, oil and water. To prevent spoilage from humidity and pests, the food was placed in a dry, well-ventilated place on racks that did not touch the floor. In some forts the soldiers kept cats to catch mice and rats and to serve as mascots.

The kitchen staff also included a baker. Bread was the main diet staple for the soldiers. Bakeries were located on the barracks' main level, near the kitchen and the flour storage. The bakeries were equipped with coal ovens where the bread was baked, along with a kneading machine and cooling-storage racks. Water for the kneading machine was heated by a boiler. The ovens were manufactured by Lespinasse or Lamoureaux. A 24-hour supply of bread was stored on wooden racks, typically 750g per man per day.

A religious service for French soldiers inside Fort Douaumont, date unknown. Note the words that appear above the small arch: 'Better to perish under the ruins of the fort than to surrender it.' (US Library of Congress)

Water was critical to the survival of the garrison. Each soldier was allotted five litres of water per day for personal use (drinking, personal sanitation and washing clothes). For washing, large troughs in masonry were provided for the men. The water was not heated. Water was also needed for cooking, cleaning, cooling the machine guns and cleaning the gun barrels. Water was stored in masonry cisterns in the lower level of the fort. The cisterns were filled by pumps or by rainwater that was filtered through the earth above the barracks and flowed through iron pipes to the cistern. Water facilities were maintained by specialists. The soldiers' latrines were primitive, being simply a hole in the floor. The officers' latrines were separate from the soldiers' and were more comfortable and private. During wartime, when the soldiers were isolated from the barracks area, portable galvanized steel containers were used.

A fortress garrison differed in many ways from a field unit. Each soldier was trained to man any post in the fort. If a fort was surrounded there was little chance for reinforcements to replace a particular need. Therefore, infantrymen were trained to work in the artillery and machine-gun turrets and in other combat locations throughout the fort, such as the counterscarp casemates or observation posts.

Life in the forts during battle could be gruelling. The men were under constant stress from the unrelenting bombardment, but they were still expected to carry on the same daily tasks as they did during times of peace. Life in Fort Moulainville, as told by its commander, Capitaine Harispe provides an insight into daily life inside the forts during battle. What follows are excerpts from Capitaine Harispe's reports to high command:

July 1916. Capitaine Harispe reports a total of 5,270 shells have fallen on the fort since the beginning of the bombardment on 26 February, including 330 from 42cm and 220 from 30.5cm and 21cm guns. All of the earthen structures on the exterior are torn up and the slopes are no longer distinguishable. The

Access shaft to the Travaux 17 tunnels at Fort Moulainville, viewed from below. This shaft drops 15m below the fort. It was carved out at the height of the battle, beginning in April 1916. The walls were later reinforced with concrete. (Julie & Cedric Vaubourg, www.fortiffsere.fr)

concrete and masonry is exposed. The infantry parapets no longer exist except for a small section. He describes the fort as having the appearance of a solidified raging sea. The armoured turrets and observation posts have taken direct hits and much damage from the large shells. The underground galleries were only 1m underground and the concrete is cracked. However, repairs must constantly be carried out.

Throughout July the pounding of Moulainville continues. The fort responds with fire from the 155mm and 75mm turrets directed at Fort Vaux, which had fallen to the Germans in early June, especially on the gorge front, the most vulnerable place. On 21 July the fort receives orders to keep up their fire on Fort Vaux. An enemy advance towards Fort Souville was expected and Moulainville would become a dangerous salient and an attack on the fort was expected from the north. In case the enemy penetrates inside the fort, defences were being organized similar to those undertaken at Fort Vaux. The men place sandbag barricades in the underground passages with embrasures for machine guns and slots to toss grenades into the corridors from behind the barricade.

One evening the fort receives a visit from the division chaplain de Poncheville who wished to speak to the men. They gather in the central corridor of the fort. The priest stands on a box of bullets and speaks in a soft voice that reaches the hearts of the men. He speaks of wandering daily throughout the French-occupied sector and he is particularly moved by the courage and endurance of the men during the long bombardments. He talks about the many conversations he has had with men from the part of France that has been invaded and is now occupied, and how this land still has a place in their heart. They look forward to a final victory. The visit raises the hopes of the men and he promises to return again soon.

In early August the bombardment picks up its intensity, in particular on the 1st when a violent barrage of 30.5cm and 42cm shells falls within a relatively short period of time. The men are evacuated into the lower tunnels; however, the fort's turret gun continues to fire on Fort Vaux. In the coming days the bombardment continues but at a slower pace. It picks up again on the 15th and several men are killed and wounded by the 42cm shells. Another particularly violent day is 21 August. The men now move to the new underground shelters in a rapid, orderly fashion, glad to be away from the violence above and protected from the asphyxiating gas by the excellent ventilation system in the tunnels.

The bombardment from those August days causes a lot of damage to the fort and repairs are undertaken whenever possible and continue into September. An inspection reveals that the ceilings of three casemates in the barracks are sagging and that the tunnel leading to the machine-gun turret is breached, as is the central gallery and the tunnel leading to the 155mm turret. The concrete around the 155mm turret is broken up and one of the armoured wedges surrounding the turret housing is out of position, impeding the action of the turret. Sacks filled with earth are placed on top of the turret for protection and the decision is made to repair the concrete. The debris in the tunnels and in front of the wartime entrance is cleared. At the end of September a cement mixer is set up in the entry vestibule of the fort and during the next several nights repairs on the concrete around the 155mm turret are

carried out. The cement is mixed then carried down the central gallery and out to the top of the fort to the outer housing of the turret. While the work party comes under occasional shelling no one is injured. It takes 27 nights to finish the repairs.

THE SITE IN WAR

In August 1914 the key Belgian fortresses of Liège and Namur fell to the Germans after being reduced by German heavy siege artillery, one fort at a time. Shortly thereafter, Fort Manonviller, east of Lunéville, the strongest and most modern fort in France, also fell to the heavy guns. In September the French fortresses of Lille, Maubeuge and Longwy fell. In late October the Belgian National Redoubt of Antwerp surrendered after German siege artillery broke through its ring of forts. The 30.5 and 42cm howitzers were the German Army's 'secret weapons', with a destructive capability unforeseen by the fortress engineers. The opening weeks of World War I brought harsh judgement on the performance of French and Belgian fortifications, an effect that would be felt in the coming months, especially at Verdun.

When the war started, Général Michel Coutanceau was governor of Verdun. The fortress under his command (which included Fort Génicourt, 15km south of Verdun) was at that time garrisoned by 63,000 soldiers and 1,400 officers, 51,000 of them combat troops. The fortress' permanent defences consisted of 12 forts, 27 intermediate infantry works, 118 artillery batteries, 26 intermediate depots, eight sector magazines and 34 combat shelters. Total firepower was 427 artillery pieces in the forts and the intervals, 268 machine guns (58 in the forts), 86 mortars and 203 revolving cannon, plus a reserve of 258 cannon, 50 mortars and eight machine guns. Verdun was extremely powerful but the destruction of the Belgian and French fortresses would have severe consequences for its future.

A note dated 5 August 1915, written by Général Benoît of the French High Command, stated that: 'A place invested rapidly consumed ammunition and supplies. If captured, the materials left behind could be captured by the enemy. In these conditions the defence of the territory depended exclusively on the field army.' Therefore, the armaments of the forts must be given to the field army. This order stripped Verdun of the massive firepower it boasted a year before. The fortress was designated the 'Fortified Region of Verdun' and all fortress and artillery troops became part of the field army. Beginning in October, infantry munitions and 75mm guns were removed from the forts to be sent to the Champagne and Argonne sectors. The guns in the turrets were left because they could not operate in the field. The forts were also emptied of their garrisons, leaving behind a small crew to fire the turret guns. This seemed a good strategy at the time, as the forts no longer played a key military role. However, in the opening days of the battle of Verdun this strategy was revealed to be a mistake.

The French Army expected an attack on Verdun at the end of 1915. When it came, the Army planned to destroy the remaining offensive and defensive capabilities of the forts so they could not be used by the Germans, as mentioned in Général Benôit's note. The order was given to place explosives throughout the forts, prepared for detonation at a moment's notice in case of a German approach. Explosive charges were placed in the turrets, Bourges and counterscarp casemates, ditches and shelters. Fort Douaumont alone was rigged with 5,000kg of black powder and 700 explosive primers. Preparations for demolition were completed by the end of January 1916.

The objective of General Erich von Falkenhayn, the German Chief of the General Staff, as stated in his post-war memoirs, in launching a large-scale offensive at Verdun was to cause the French to mount an equally massive defence, and in so doing, attrit and reduce the size and morale of the French Army. The loss of the symbolic town of Verdun would be a huge blow to the French and could possibly open up the gap in the French front needed to allow German forces to roll up the entire French line and win the war in the west. The plan was to rapidly break through the defences of the right bank and capture Verdun, driving the French into retreat. With such a large number of forces put into the attack (150,000 men) and the equally massive and devastating bombardment planned, Falkenhayn expected a quick victory.

A German 42cm 'Big Bertha' howitzer emplaced north of Verdun in early 1916. Although very successful against Belgian forts in 1914 and Russian forts in 1915, at Verdun the 42cm howitzer found its match in the more modern French forts, especially Fort Douaumont. (Marc Romanych collection)

This is the oft-heard 'bleed the French white' explanation. In reality it was simpler. In 1915 the Germans seized a bridgehead over the Meuse at Saint-Mihiel. This action cut off the railway line to Verdun and surrounded it on three sides. The only supply route into the fortress was a single, small road. If the Germans could cut that road the fortress could not be resupplied and it would quickly fall. This military reality plus the weakened fortifications are more likely reasons why Verdun was chosen for the offensive.

A massive and historic artillery bombardment began on 21 February against the forward French positions. One million shells fell in the first 10 hours. When the bombardment lifted, German assault formations of the 5. Armee, consisting of III, VII and XVIII Armee Korps, advanced. The offensive was directed by German Crown Prince Wilhelm. His Chief of Staff, General Schmidt von Knobelsdorf, exercised tactical control. Despite the preparatory shelling the lead formations encountered stubborn French resistance. The advance slowed but the French lines began to cave in. The key to the right-bank defences, Fort Douaumont, fell on 25 February and both sides expected that the fall of Verdun was imminent.

The fall of Fort Douaumont

German gunners had fired 62 shells from their 42cm howitzers at the fort. Despite the 42's extraordinary power and ability to crack even the toughest concrete, the fort had held up rather well. The story of the bizarre capture of Fort Douaumont is well told. A small band of German pioneers attached to Brandenburgisches Infanterie-Regiment 24 approached the fort on the morning of 25 February and found it virtually undefended. The fort's observers had been driven underground by the German bombardment and the fort's armoured observation posts were unmanned. The pioneers passed through the fence and into the ditch surrounding the fort, climbed inside the north-east ditch casemate and from there advanced into the interior. The small French garrison was surprised and quickly surrendered. On 22 May an assault to recapture the fort was led by Général Charles Mangin with three divisions. The three-day assault ended in failure and huge French losses. Two more offensives were launched by Mangin's 5e Division on 22 April and 22 May.

The ditch of Fort Douaumont, showing the north-west flanking casemate. Remnants of the counterscarp wall appear on the left and the escarp is to the right. In the centre are fragments of the iron fence from the base of the escarp. (National Archives of the US)

The German attack on the right-bank forts of Verdun

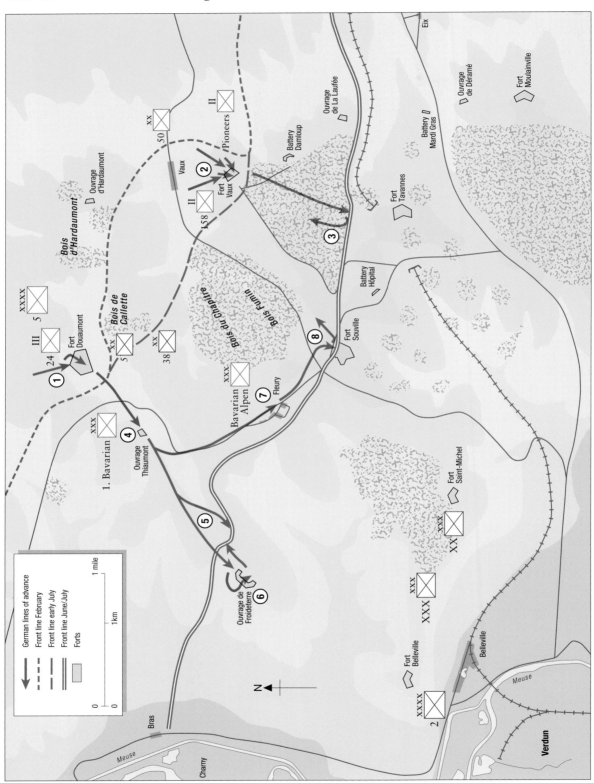

Both resulted in French troops reaching the fort, including the capture of a Bourges casemate, but they were driven off and the offensives failed.

In 1914 the size of Fort Douaumont's garrison was 500 soldiers, but in February 1916 it was just 56. Word of the capture quickly spread in both French and German circles. Although the capture was reported by the French Army as a loss after a 'fierce struggle and many fruitless assaults' by the Germans, needless to say it was a shock to France and to the soldiers on the battlefield. French troops, after seeing the German signal flag waving on top of the fort, went into a panic and started to retreat. On 26 February Général Herr, who had replaced Coutanceau as military governor of Verdun, gave the order to destroy Fort Vaux. However, the German bombardment had already destroyed the explosive charges before they were put in place and armed. Fortunately, Général Henri-Phillipe Pétain, commander of the French 2e Armée south of Verdun, was given command of the defence of Verdun by Général Joffre, Commander-in-Chief of the French Army, on the same day. Pétain arrived on the scene and restored calm. Where Général Herr saw chaos, Pétain saw possibilities. The situation was grim but Verdun was still in French hands and only one fort had fallen. Pétain gave the order to resist in place and to remove the explosive charges from the forts. He believed that Verdun had the best chance to survive by restoring the forts to their former powerful conditions. Fort Douaumont had fallen too easily and its loss was a blow to

the defences. He immediately ordered the artillery returned to the forts and the garrisons resupplied, and set up a *position de barrage* along the principal line of resistance and a 'line of panic' on the former line of sustainment. Général Balfourier's XX 'Iron' Corps also arrived on the 26th and two additional corps were on the way. For the time being the German offensive on the right bank came to a halt.

Fort Vaux

The German 5. Armee launched a second offensive on the right bank in late May, after some success on the left bank from March to May. Using three corps with five divisions, the objective was to seize the Thiaumont works, the Fleury Ridge and Fort Souville in order to gain 'bases of departure' from which to launch a final drive into Verdun. The initial objective was Fort Vaux, which had already repulsed German attacks in April and May. The 1st and 7th German divisions launched an attack against Fort Vaux on 1 June. Their initial thrust into the Bois Fumin brought them to within 1,000m of the fort. There they prepared for an early morning surprise attack on the fort.

Structurally, Fort Vaux was a wreck. Mentally, the defenders inside the fort were in a similar state. The fort had been pounded by both large- and medium-calibre guns. In February a 42cm shell set off demolition charges placed by the French, destroying the fort's only 75mm turret. Now the fort's only serviceable weapons were machine guns. The shelling had also breached the concrete shell of the fort, exposing the interior passages. Some underground galleries were cracked and, worst of all, the cisterns were leaking, allowing most of the fort's water supplies to drain away.

Major Sylvain-Eugene Raynal took command of the fort on 24 May. He found the soldiers of the garrison packed together in the corridors, in no position to offer any resistance if an attack should come. Even worse, the fort was in the path of French soldiers fleeing the German attack in that sector, and was looked upon as a haven. When the Germans attacked, the garrison stood at 600 men in a fort capable of supporting 250 with adequate water supplies, which Fort Vaux no longer had. Raynal commented in his biography how, upon his initial inspection of the fort, it would have been appropriate to hang a sign over the entry quoting from Dante's *Inferno*: 'Abandon hope, all ye who enter here.'

The ditch on the south-west side of Fort Vaux. Nothing remains of the counterscarp or escarp walls (see Plate B on p. 21). The retaining wall of the Bourges casemate appears to the left. (Author's collection)

The superstructure of Fort Douaumont. Capitaine Harispe, commander of the fort after its recapture, repaired the fort and added the planking along the paths. The large craters are from German 42cm shells. (US Library of Congress)

The Germans sent two battalions from the 50. Infanterie-Division to capture the fort. They took position in trenches below the front of the fort and proceeded across the glacis into the ditch under fire from the machine guns on top and then from the counterscarp casemates. Pioneers advanced to the top of the north-east casemate and attempted to lower grenades into the embrasures. The Germans finally gained access to the inside and the defenders of the casemate surrendered.

The Germans simultaneously attacked the casemate in the north-west corner. When the guns of the casemate momentarily stopped firing a small company of troops from the 158th Paderborn Regiment ran across the ditch and up the escarp to the top of the fort where they came under fire from Fort Moulainville's 155mm turret, still active despite the shelling the fort was taking. The north-west casemate machine guns began firing again, stranding the Paderborners on top of the fort. The German pioneers managed to get through a sandbag barricade blocking a breach and tossed grenades inside the casemate. The French evacuated the casemate through tunnels that led to the main part of the fort.

Now that both casemates had fallen, the Germans proceeded down the galleries to gain access to the main part of the fort. In the north-east corridor the pioneers came across a steel door blocking the corridor. They used grenades, the only explosives they had with them at the time, to blow their way through the door. Raynal and his men had set up sandbags and a machine gun farther down the corridor to block the German advance.

By the next day, 2 June, the Germans had completely encircled the fort, blocking any French escape. The main battle continued in the dark tunnels but the Germans made no progress and tried a different technique for subduing the fort. On this same day Raynal sent out a message via carrier pigeon asking for a French counter-attack to relieve the fort. This was carried out by the 124th Division on 4 June. The French reached the western edge of the fort but six waves of attacks were driven off by the Düsseldorf Fusiliers and the effort was abandoned. Later that day the Germans returned to the fort with six flame-thrower crews in an attempt to rain fire on every available opening they could find. Thick black smoke poured through the tunnels. The defenders in the tunnels fell back but, when the Germans halted their flame attack to

advance, the defenders returned to the machine guns. All available vents were opened in order to clear the smoke. The Germans attacked the south-west corner casemate but the French counter-attacked, capturing the German flame-throwers.

On 4 June Raynal received news of the cracked cisterns and that the men had only a small amount of water left, not enough to last much longer. The four-day battle had so far resulted in disaster for the Germans, as they had captured only a small part of the tunnel system, but the French situation was equally grim.

The Germans' bad luck continued on the 5th. They attempted to dig down from the top of the fort into the tunnels but were driven off by a French bombardment. They blew a hole into the south-west Bourges casemate and attacked the inside with a flame-thrower but the air currents from inside the fort blew the flame back into their faces and they had to retreat. The Germans began to think the fort could not be captured, but a chain of events took place on 7 June that led its surrender.

Many of the men inside were sick or wounded. A French counter-attack on 6 June gave them hope but they watched as it too failed. Finally the water ran out. Morale in the fort had collapsed despite Raynal's efforts. He managed to signal Souville one last time requesting immediate relief but it was not forthcoming. Shells were now raining in, collapsing the central gallery. Raynal decided it was time to surrender. In the battle for Fort Vaux, the French suffered about 100 casualties with 20 killed. The Germans lost 2,678 men and 64 officers. The battle revealed the difficulties of an assault on a fort, even one deprived of its original defences. It should also be noted that the counter-attacks on Forts Vaux and Douaumont had cost the French thousands of casualties.

After the fall of Fort Vaux the Germans could now advance towards their next objective – the line of sustainment, and in particular Fort Souville. Their left flank headed towards Fort Tavannes, but was unable to make any headway towards its capture as they had run into a French force headed towards the relief of Fort Vaux. The I Königlich Bayerische Armee Korps on the right flank moved down the Thiaumont ridge towards the Thiaumont intermediate infantry works that stood halfway between Fort Douaumont and the Froideterre Works. From this point the Thiaumont ridge bisected the Fleury ridge that ran through the village of Fleury towards Fort Souville. The Thiaumont works commanded the Fleury ridge. On 8 June the Thiaumont works fell but were quickly retaken by the French. The position would change hands more than a dozen times over the summer.

The main German attack began on 23 June, with a force of 30,000 men. The Bavarians overran the Thiaumont works and moved down the ridge towards Froideterre. They captured the Four Chimneys shelter and PC119 (originally designated Shelter FT2), which were serving as command posts, and surrounded Froideterre.

F **THE INITIAL ATTACK ON FORT VAUX, 1 JUNE 1916**

On 1 June 1916 two groups of pioneers set out in the direction of the north-east and north-west casemates. They lowered and tossed grenades into the embrasures of the casemates, which surrendered later in the day, allowing the Germans to penetrate the tunnels below the fort. When the machine guns in the north-west casemate jammed, several soldiers from the 158th Paderborn Regiment ran across the ditch to the top of the fort. They came under fire from a French machine gun but remained on top until 3 June. The battle continued until the French surrendered on 7 June.

The Froideterre Works

The brief battle that took place at the Froideterre Works on 23 June turned the tide of the battle in favour of the French and proved the value of a fully defended fort. Had the Germans succeeded in surpassing the Froideterre Works they would have broken through the fortress line and moved towards the town of Verdun only 4km away.

Froideterre held a key position at the end of the Thiaumont ridge. It consisted of four unconnected combat blocks surrounded by a shallow ditch with no flanking protection. Its weapons consisted of a 75mm armoured turret, two machine-gun turrets and a Bourges casemate for two 75mm cannon. Fortunately for the defending French soldiers, Froideterre was restored to its pre-August 1915 fighting capacity, with a full garrison and supplies. Froideterre was commanded by Capitaine Dartigues. He knew the value of fortifications and how to set up a good defence. This knowledge proved to be priceless. Dartigues set up interior defences consisting of machine-gun positions in the entrances to the barracks and the 75mm block.

At 0800hrs on 23 June the Germans approached the fort, in the words of Capitaine Dartigues, 'with their hands in their pockets, thinking Froideterre [fallen]'. The alert was given and Dartigues set up his command post behind the machine-gun position at the main entrance. At 0930hrs the Germans had reached the ditch. The machine-gun turret defending the glacis behind the barracks became jammed by debris that had fallen between the turret and the housing and it could not turn to fire. The Germans came around to the rear of the fort and the machine gun in the barracks opened fire, sending the Germans for cover on top. They tossed a grenade inside a breach in the wall of the barracks made by a 30.5cm shell, which then set off a small stock of fuses. Thinking the French would now evacuate the fort, the Germans moved back around to the rear. The machine gun opened fire again and the Germans moved back on top of the fort. In a short time they again returned to the rear, moving from crater to crater for shelter. Dartigues sent a courier to the 75mm block, ordering his men to fire shrapnel and pellet charges on the attackers. The 75mm gun fired 116 rounds at the Germans, who were forced to run for cover. A French infantry counter-attack followed, chasing the Germans back up the ridge. The fighting at Froideterre ended.

Despite German efforts, the June offensive slowed to a halt. The tide was now beginning to turn in France's favour. The Germans were also feeling the effects of the heat and were thirsty. Falkenhayn began to sense defeat, but Knobelsdorf asked Prince Wilhelm for one more attempt to break through. This next attack was scheduled for early July.

On 10 July the Germans unleashed this second attack, which proceeded once again towards Fort Souville. On 12 July a small German force reached the glacis of the fort and, for the first time since February, a German soldier spotted the towers of the cathedral of Verdun in the valley below. It would be their last glimpse of the town. They had no support behind them and the French launched a sortie out of the fort to chase them off. The French counter-attack drove the Germans back to their starting point of 10 July. The fighting continued for the next few weeks, and it took an entire French battalion to recapture PC119 on the Thiaumont ridge. By now it was evident that the Germans were defeated and the French were on the move.

Général Nivelle, placed in command of 2e Armée on 1 May, after Pétain was named commander of the Armée de Centre (Pétain had been essentially relieved of duty by Général de Castelnau of the French High Command for his ineffectiveness from March to May), now set about planning the offensive to retake the right bank. His primary objective was Fort Douaumont. To facilitate its recapture Nivelle would turn the tables on the Germans by bringing up French heavy guns to pound the fort. The gun in question was the Schneider-Creusot 400mm railway gun.

Fort Douaumont in October

The Germans occupying Fort Douaumont believed themselves to be protected from the French 18cm and 22cm shells, as they had withstood the French shelling over the last eight months. On 18 October the shelling increased in intensity, surpassing previous bombardments. According to a German witness, the casemates trembled, all openings in the fort to the outside were demolished and the observatories cracked. The Germans were unable to move. The shelling increased on the 20th, shaking the fort continuously.

The Schneider-Creusot 400mm railway gun. Six shots from this gun on Fort Douaumont on 23 October 1916 ignited a munitions depot deep within the fort and caused it to surrender. The gun in this photograph is being fired by US soldiers. (National Archives of the US)

Barracks of Fort Douaumont. Concrete was added to the masonry façade but was mostly chipped away by German and French bombardments in 1916. This photograph was taken in 1918 by US forces. (US Library of Congress)

A French attack was expected at any moment and the garrison of 400 German troops was ready to repel any assault on the fort.

The bombardment once again increased in intensity on the 23rd. The Germans were waiting in the corridors and casemates when suddenly at 1230hrs an enormous blast was heard like none before. Thunder shook the centre of the fort, caused by the first shell from the French 400mm railway gun. The huge shell struck the infirmary, killing everyone inside. Ten minutes later a second shell completely destroyed casemate number eight. Every ten minutes the 400mm shells struck the fort, destroying casemates 10, 11 and 17. The men were evacuated to the lower level. The sixth shot was fatal. It passed through the floor into the lower level, exploding in the engineer's depot. Flames spread throughout the lower level, igniting machine-gun munitions and fuses. A stock of grenades and French shells were stored in the room adjacent to the depot, so the German commander, Major Rosendahl, fearing these would explode next, ordered the evacuation of the fort, leaving behind a small force of firefighters. For hours the wounded were moved out of the fort to the rear and a procession continued into the early hours of the morning. Behind them smoke poured out of every opening in the fort as the fire in the depot raged on. On 24 October a small group of Germans remained in the fort to fight the fire.

The capture of Fort Douaumont was assigned to Général de Salin's 38e Division composed of two battalions of French colonial troops, Bataillons Croll and Nicolai; these were very tough men feared by the Germans. The morning of 24 October was foggy and the French proceeded slowly towards the fort, losing their bearings in the fog. Lost in the fog, around 1440hrs, Capitaine Nicolai finally discovered where they were and headed in the direction of the fort. The fog momentarily parted and a shaft of sun miraculously fell through, illuminating the top of Fort Douaumont. The battalion moved forward. A patrol of the 133e Régiment d'Infanterie, commanded by Caporal Barranguier, reached the top of the fort first. Nicolai's battalion encountered only light resistance, and the fort was once again in French hands. Observers

G   WAITING TO ATTACK

Capitaine Nicolai's battalion of the Régiment d'Infanterie Coloniale du Maroc (Colonial Infantry Regiment of Morocco) wait to storm and recapture Fort Douaumont, 24 October 1916. The regiment approached the fort but became lost in the dense fog that blanketed the battlefield. Suddenly, at around 1430hrs, the fog parted and the sun shone down revealing the top of the fort. The men were joyous and within the hour it was back in French hands after eight long months.

at Fort Souville were also watching in the direction of the fort. The fog parted for the observers and they could see French soldiers waving their arms on top of the fort, a glorious sight to behold. The French quickly moved to the interior, where about 40 German defenders under Hauptmann Prollius surrendered after about 15 minutes.

Later German testimony revealed that the fort was still capable of resisting an attack until the bombardment by the 400mm shells had breached the lower level of the fort and ignited the munitions in the depot. The French guns had, since 18 October, also maintained an accurate fire on all the fort's exits, making reinforcement impossible. The recapture of Fort Douaumont was a huge French victory.

The number of casualties sustained during the battle of Verdun differs based on the sources. Later French estimates put the casualties at 420,000 dead and 800,000 gassed or wounded. France's official history of the war puts the number of French casualties (dead, wounded or missing) at 377,321 (162,308 dead or missing), with 337,000 Germans killed or wounded. A total of 150,000 unidentified corpses were collected and interred at the Douaumont Ossuary.

AFTERMATH

The Travaux 1917 tunnels below Fort Moulainville. This photograph shows the tunnels carved into the limestone with steel beam supports above and wooden shoring beams along the walls. (Julie & Cedric Vaubourg, www.fortiffsere.fr)

After the war ended, French military engineers re-examined the decisions that led to the order of 5 August 1915 to dismantle the forts, and the debate continued for many years thereafter. First of all, the notion that the artillery removed from the forts would make a difference in the field was false. Stripping the forts of their armament provided only a small number of pieces relative to the actual need of the field army, and the design of the fortress artillery carriages made them difficult for field service. However, a worse consequence was the weakened state of the key positions of Forts Douaumont and Vaux. Could the overall weakened state of Verdun have helped the Germans decide to make Verdun the target of their 1916 offensive? Possibly. In hindsight, the dismantling of the forts was a clear error. The lack of firepower allowed the Germans to quickly overrun the first line of resistance, gain a foothold on the right bank and quickly capture Fort Douaumont. For eight months, Fort Douaumont provided an excellent vantage point for the Germans to observe the French positions, and it could shelter at any given time over 1,000 German soldiers.

After the battle of Verdun, modifications continued in the most important forts, and this would influence the future design of French fortifications, the Maginot Line in particular. This was called the 'Travaux 17' or '[19]17 Works'. Construction began officially during the battle at Fort Moulainville. The fort had taken a tremendous pounding during the battle, including many hits by the German 42cm howitzers. The danger was

so great and disturbing to the men that they had had to leave the fort during the bombardment to hide in nearby trenches, and return at night when the bombardment subsided. The commander of the fort, Capitaine Harispe, and his staff, Commandants Dosse and Delage, were looking for a solution that would allow the soldiers to remain in the fort under adequate protection. Dosse and Delage came up with the idea of digging down into the limestone below the fort to carve out bomb-proof tunnels and rooms where the garrison could escape during the shelling. The concept worked, giving the soldiers a safe haven from the bombing. The idea was introduced to the Army command and authorized to be carried out at other forts. The following forts were considered of primary importance and given priority: Douaumont, Moulainville, Rozelier, Haudainville, Déramé and La Falouse.

The primary objectives of the modernization and reorganization programme was to respond to three successive types of defensive situation: defending the superstructure, defending the entryways and defending the underground galleries. The first step was to reduce the number of ways to get into the fort. Entries were barricaded and chicanes were set up with machine-gun embrasures and grenade sumps. New underground galleries were dug out, accessible by shafts. The shafts ranged in depth from 5 to 15m, depending on the ground above, whether rock or earth. The shafts permitted the garrison to access underground command posts, barracks, food supplies, munitions, water wells, kitchens and latrines. They also provided safe access to the turrets and casemates. Electric lights were installed and in some tunnels heating ducts were added. The new underground system was connected by tunnels to rear entrances outside the perimeter of the fort, allowing the soldiers to escape if the fort came under siege. The rear entries were camouflaged and placed on the rear slopes of hills. A new ventilation system was tested at Forts Belrupt and Souville and the La Laufée works, which created an overpressure inside the fort to keep out poison gas. Outside air was pumped through filters before entering the fort. These modifications fulfilled three principles later used in the Maginot Line – deep shelter below the earth, dispersion of the combat elements and a remote entrance far to the rear. The 1917 modifications were approved for the entire fortress system. A total of 34km of tunnels and shafts were dug out by November 1918.

A Pamart casemate for two machine guns. Located to the rear of Fort Souville. (Author's collection)

Additional work was done on the damaged forts to repair the breaches and destruction caused by the German bombardment. Concrete machine-gun positions were built into the damaged façades of the forts.

In September 1916 the French began to install a new type of machine-gun casemate on the flanks of the forts. A number of different models were tested and the final model selected was designed by Capitaine Pamart. One model had a single embrasure and the other, the most common, had two. It became known as the 'Pamart' casemate. Resembling an elephant's eyes and trunk, it was protected by a 6–14cm-thick armoured plate of molded steel that could withstand 22cm shells. The roof was curved to deflect incoming fire. It was equipped with a pair of Saint Étienne model-1907 machine guns. The carriage was built so the guns could be pulled out of one embrasure and moved to the other as needed or to allow one gun to cool down while the other fired. The guns had a firing angle of 90 degrees. The embrasures could be blocked with shutters for protection and a hand-operated ventilator was provided to

American soldiers from Patton's Third Army visit Fort Douaumont in 1944. In the centre is the armoured observation post and the concrete cylinder that protects it. In the background is the Galopin 155R gun turret. (National Archives of the US)

clear the air of fumes. The ensemble was built by the Ferry-Capitain company, was 80cm high and weighed 3.7 tons. Several of the Pamart casemates were connected by tunnel to the Travaux 17 shelters. A total of 34 were placed at Verdun, 26 of these with double embrasures. The new casemates were included in the Travaux 17 as part of a concept of 'machine-gun tentacles'. These were tunnels branching out from the centre of the fort and outside the perimeter to the new machine-gun casemates. Three were placed around Fort Souville and around the less-threatened forts, and in some fortified works of the first line such as Froideterre, Douaumont, Vaux and La Laufée.

In early 1917 the Germans dug a new defensive line around Verdun. On the left bank under the hill named Mort Homme, the Germans dug three 500m-long tunnels (named Bismark, Galwitz and Kronprinz) to protect their supplies and command post. They also built a number of strong field fortifications along the line. Meanwhile the French dug new forward lines on the heights of the Meuse. Over the next few months they were able to recapture several key positions. In September 1918 the American Expeditionary Force under General Pershing began its Meuse–Argonne offensive to reduce the Saint-Mihiel salient and capture the Argonne Forest. On 26 September the Americans attacked between the Argonne Forest and Montfaucon and were able to surround the enemy positions by the 28th. Fighting to the north of Verdun continued right up until the Armistice of 11 November.

Ironically, on 14 June 1940 the Germans stood once again in front of Verdun. There was brief fighting but at 1145hrs on 15 June Fort Douaumont surrendered without a shot fired. Just 15 minutes later Fort Vaux also surrendered.

THE SITE TODAY

No battlefield in France, and perhaps in all of Europe, is more sacred than Verdun. No patch of land on earth the size of the right-bank sector of Verdun took more of a beating. Eyewitness accounts and stereoscopic photos show a lunar landscape left behind by the shelling. Practically every square metre

The glacis of the Froideterre Works showing craters from heavy bombardment in 1916. At the base is the shallower 'triangular' ditch. The machine-gun turret guarding this sector jammed, allowing the Bavarians to cross the escarp slope and attack the French in the barracks located to the left. (Author's collection)

of land was affected in one way or another. For years the battlefield was a graveyard; most of the remains were never identified and were buried according to where they were found. It is a place where unexploded shells are still uncovered. In the 1920s and 30s new trees were planted on the hills and ravines of the old battlefield. Today Verdun is a beautiful, peaceful landscape of forests and ravines. However, it is also an eerie place. From the road one sees the forest but beneath the undergrowth are the remnants of shell craters and trenches, a reminder of what once was and could be if the brush and the trees were removed. Above all, Verdun is a memorial. Visitors can see the battle sites and memorials scattered throughout, crowned by the huge Douaumont Ossuary, the 'Place of Bones'.

Access to the battlefield is well marked from all directions. The E50/A4 is the main autoroute that runs past Verdun to the south. From the east (the direction of Metz) the road crosses the flat Woevre Plain then climbs through the hills between Fort Rozelier and the Ouvrage de Saint-Symphorien. After it crosses the Meuse south of Fort Haudainville it continues past Fort Dugny to the south and Fort Landrecourt to the north then on towards the Argonne Forest.

To visit the town of Verdun, use exit 31 at Haudainville and head into town on the D964. Below Haudainville, the D964 runs along the river Meuse to Toul, Saint-Mihiel and the forts between Toul and Verdun to the east of the Meuse (Troyon, Génicourt). The D964 also runs south to Verdun from the direction of Stenay and Dun. The D903 runs alongside the autoroute and the D603 runs from Verdun through the battlefield on the right bank towards Abocourt. For the most interesting way to reach the right-bank battlefields from the direction of Metz via the autoroute, take the Fresnes-en-Woevre exit and head south on the D908 for about 1km then right on the D903. Before reaching the first hills of the right bank there is a road that is accessible from the D903 north of Haudiomont that runs towards Ronvaux, Watronville, Châtillon-sous-les-Côtes, Moulainville, Eix, Damloup and Vaux. From the town of Verdun, stay on the D964 to the D112 and then the D603. Follow the signs to the 'Champs de Bataille'.

The main battlefield sites on the right bank are Forts Vaux, Douaumont and Froideterre, the destroyed village of Fleury, the Mémorial de Verdun and the Douaumont Ossuary, plus some of the smaller batteries and interval works (Hôpital, Damloup and Thiaumont). These are all clearly marked with direction signs. The best place to start is the Mémorial de Verdun. This is both a museum and the battlefield's visitors' centre. It contains hundreds of relics and photos, a large map presentation showing the stages of the battle and an excellent bookstore with maps and guidebooks.

While some of the fortifications on the right bank can be visited, many are on private or military property. To the south-west of the memorial building, deep in the woods, is Fort Souville. Parking is available just beyond the lion memorial on the corner. A walking trail leads from the car park to a Pamart casemate. Farther down the road is a dirt trail leading off to the west, on the south flank of Fort Souville. There are some excellent sites to see along this trail, including a munitions depot and the experimental Bussière 155mm turret. Next to the turret is another Pamart casemate and the remnants of an interval artillery battery. Fort Souville itself is located deeper in the woods. It is off limits and very difficult to reach.

On the north side of the memorial is the Thiaumont ridge, along which runs the Froideterre Works, the Four Chimneys shelter, the Thiaumont works, PC 118 and 119, the Douaumont Ossuary and, at the end of the road, Fort

Douaumont. The grounds around the forts are free of trees and vegetation and are clearly visible. At the end of the ridge beyond Froideterre are some interval infantry shelters including the combat shelters MF1 and MF2. Froideterre itself is a spectacular site to see. Inside the main structure are the barracks casemates with the newer-model metal bunks for the troops. A short tunnel leads to the machine-gun turret and observatory. The 75mm casemate is in a separate location, as is the Bourges casemate on the left flank. The perimeter of the fort is cleared of vegetation and the ditch and shell craters are visible. Little remains of the Thiaumont works except for some twisted metal and concrete. Fort Douaumont, on the other hand, is in very good shape inside, despite the pounding it took during the war. The casemates can be visited on the upper and lower levels. One of the casemates is set up with beds and a stove. The lower level leads to the washrooms and the munitions magazines. In the centre is the shaft leading to the Travaux 17 tunnels that run below the fort. This is a large pit about 15m² with a ladder running down in two corners of the fort. The depth of the shaft is 36m. The lower tunnels are not accessible. The fort's 155mm Galopin turret can be visited. The size of the turret and the housing is immense; the visitor can stroll on the top of the fort and get some excellent views of the plain to the east and the battlefield to the rear. One can clearly see the strategic value of this position as an observatory. Fort Vaux is also open for visits. Scenes have been set up with mannequins showing the appearance of the inside of the fort during the battle. Guided visits are also available.

Douaumont Ossuary should be left for last. This imposing building with a central tower in the shape of an artillery shell can be seen from most of the battlefield. The tower is 46m high and the wings are 137m long. Parking is available at the rear of the building. As one approaches the building, a shocking scene presents itself. At the base of the wings that spread out on either side of the central tower are small windows. Behind each window are the skeletal remains of the men found across the battlefield. Skulls, leg bones and pelvic bones assault the viewer with this vision of the true horror of Verdun. The bones are piled in chambers under the floor of the ossuary. Above each chamber is a grey marble sarcophagus in an arched niche. Each niche and sarcophagus represents an area of the battlefield where the bones below the floor were found. All of the most notorious battle sites are carved into the stone above each sarcophagus. The niches run along the back wall of the building. Across from each is a stained-glass window that casts an eerie reddish/orange light. The sight is quite stunning. The ossuary also contains a small gift shop. Access to the top of the central tower offers a view over the battlefield. A traditional military cemetery lies across the road from the ossuary, with neat rows of Christian crosses and tombstones for the Jewish and Muslim soldiers killed at Verdun.

The citadel and surrounding walls in the town of Verdun are magnificent. Bastioned walls and gates surround the town and Verdun Cathedral sits on top of the hill. Most of the original works still exist, though rumour has it that they are endangered. A small section of the citadel's tunnels is open for visits. There is a small electric cart that runs along a track in the floor, like an amusement ride, stopping every few minutes in front of filmed scenes of actors playing soldiers at the time of the siege in 1916. The ride moves automatically along the corridors past replicas of bakeries and infirmaries.

There is little to see on the left bank, except for a glimpse of Fort Sartelles. Exit the town from the west and follow the Voie Sacrée (Sacred Way), on the

A remnant of the armoured collar piece that surrounded the 75mm gun turret at Fort Vaux. This particular turret exploded when it was hit by a German shell, setting off explosives placed inside by the French to sabotage the fort. (Author's collection)

D603 for a few blocks to the Rue Blamont to the right, then the Rue des Sartelles. This runs past the fort, clearly visible from the road. Since this is an Army tank-training area it is not recommended to stop here for too long. The remaining forts of the left bank are under French Army control or are privately owned. They are difficult to get to and the access roads are in bad shape. Permission must be obtained from the Army or the landowner prior to proceeding to any other forts. At this time the Ouvrage de la Falouse is being restored for visits and will be one of the best restored works at Verdun.

There are many other sites to see around Verdun. The Argonne Forest is about 25km down the road to the west. The best way to get there is to follow the D603. There one is struck by the darkness and isolation of this vast forest. Both armies dug shelters into the hills and even today not all of them have

Remains of the Ouvrage de Thiaumont, the scene of relentless fighting in June 1916. This is the armoured observatory. (Julie & Cedric Vaubourg, www.fortiffsere.fr)

Bourges casemate, the Ouvrage de Froideterre. Its two 75mm guns were aimed towards the Meuse Valley and crossed fire with the Charny works on the opposite side. (Author's collection)

been explored. The tunnels are still there but are dangerous. Along the road between Binarville and Apremont is the site of the Lost Battalion, where soldiers of the American 77th Infantry Division were surrounded for six days by the Germans. East of the Argonne Forest is the Butte de Vauquois, the site of huge mine craters blown by the French and Germans in attempts to destroy each other's forward positions near the town of Vauqois. A guided tour of the mine tunnels is possible. South of Verdun, above the village of Les Éparges, is another series of craters from the 1915 offensive.

About 12km south of Verdun is Fort Génicourt, and 6km south of that is Fort Troyon. Both are Séré de Rivières forts. Troyon is open for visits. Perhaps the best example of this type of fort is Uxegny at Épinal. The restoration work done here is magnificent and the fort is open for tours.

Entrance to the tunnels underneath the citadel of Verdun. A total of 2km of tunnels were dug to house men and munitions. (Author's collection)

For the latest information on the forts of Verdun and the Séré de Rivières in general there is a wonderful website created by Julie and Cedric Vaubourg – www.fortiffsere.fr. It contains thousands of photos of the forts, current and vintage, as well as information on forts that are open to the public.

Metz lies 60km east of Verdun. Here one can visit a restored example of the German Mostelstellung works – the Feste Wagner. It now boasts the only working 15cm gun battery in the world with all four gun turrets restored to perfect condition. Also at Metz is Fort Queuleu. This fort was built by the French in 1867. It is now an open park and numerous features of the fort can be seen from the footpaths, including the impressive entry gate.

The city of Thionville is 30km north of Metz. The German-built Fort Guentrange is open for visits of its interior, including the massive barracks and the north gun battery. Stop by the Hotel l'Horizon near the fort for dinner and a marvellous view of the valley. The Fort d'Illange, also German built, is located across the Moselle and is a public park where one can stroll along the paths by the concrete barracks, gun batteries and picket shelters. Finally, the Maginot Line runs about 30km to the north of Verdun and there are several of its works open for visits. Indeed, all of Lorraine is extraordinarily rich in military architecture and history, especially for those who study the history of fortifications.

BIBLIOGRAPHY

Albin, Michel (ed.), *Journal du Commandant Raynal – Le Fort Vaux*, Paris: Albin Michel, 1919

Association pour la Restauration du Fort d'Uxegney et la Place d'Épinal, *Le Fort d'Uxegney*, Épinal: 1995

Beumelburg, Werner, *Douaumont – Schlachten des Weltkrieges*, Oldenburg: Verlag Gerhard Stalling, 1925

Bichet, Gabriel, *Le Rôle des Forts dans la Bataille de Verdun*, Nancy: Imprimerie Georges Thomas, 1969

Denizot, Alain, *Douaumont 1914–1918, Vérité et légende*, Paris: Perrin, 1994

Frijns, Marco, Malchair, Luc, Moulins, Jean-Jacques and Puelinckx, Jean, *Index de la Fortification Française Métropole et Outre-Mer 1874–1914*, Auto-edition, 2008

Holstein, Christina, *Fort Douaumont – Verdun*, Yorkshire: Pen & Sword Books, 2002

Horne, Alistair, *The Price of Glory – Verdun 1916*, London: Penguin Books, 1962

Kaluzko, Jean-Luc and Radet, Frédéric, *1916 Verdun, Secrets d'une place forte*, Louvier: Ysec Editions, 2006

Le Hallé, Guy, *Le Système Séré de Rivières, ou le Témoignage des Pierres*, Louviers: Ysec Editions, 2001

——, *Verdun, Les forts de la Victoire*, Paris: Citédis, 1998

Marga, A., *Géographie Militaire, École de l'Artillerie & Du Génie – Cours D'Art Militaire*, Fontainbleau: 1880

Marot, Jean (ed.), *Die Schlacht von Verdun in Bildern*, Paris: Durassié Druck and Verlag, 1970

Ménager, Lieutenant R., *Les Forts de Moulainville et de Douaumont Sous les 420*, Paris: Payot, 1936

Romains, Jules, *Verdun*, New York: Alfred A. Knopf, 1939

Truttmann, Phillippe, *La Barrière de Fer – L'Architecture des Forts du Général Séré de Rivières (1872–1914)*, Luxembourg: Gerard Klopp, 2000

Tuchman, Barbara, *The Guns of August*, New York: Macmillan, 1962

GLOSSARY

Battery	A position for artillery on the rampart of a fort or in the intervals between forts.
Caponier	A work built across the ditch of a fort, on one or more levels, with embrasures to protect the ditch from an enemy attempt to infiltrate it and reach the centre of the fort.
Casemate	An armoured compartment for artillery or small arms.
Cavalier	A raised rampart on top of a fort where artillery was placed to command the surrounding area.
Counterscarp	The inside facing of the outer wall of a ditch.
Ditch	A long, narrow excavation of varying length, width and depth, built to deter an attack on the central part of a fort or smaller works. Also called a dry moat.
Escarp	The inner wall or slope across the ditch from the counterscarp.
Glacis	A gentle slope extending from a fortification designed to expose attacking enemy infantry to defenders on top of the fort.
Gorge	The rear face of the works, typically where the entrance is located.
Infantry works (*ouvrages*)	Small forts placed in the intervals of the larger forts – designed to provide coverage of places that cannot be targeted by the forts themselves, such as ravines.
Ouvrage	A military term denoting 'works', used generically to describe a type of fortification of no particular size or capability. Used throughout French military nomenclature beginning in 1910.
Parapet	An earthen or concrete embankment to protect soldiers from enemy fire.
Traverse	An earthen (or concrete) structure placed perpendicular to an artillery rampart to protect the gun platform from enfilading fire from the sides. Personnel or munitions shelters were built underneath.
Turret cap	Steel-plated covering in the shape of a skullcap that protects the gun and artillerymen inside the gun chamber of an armoured turret. The rounded shape deflects enemy shells.

INDEX